Poured Out

Phillip D Lloyd

To the believers who sincerely desire to know God and give him the complete trust of their life. I pray that the Spirit will melt away any of the blockades that have held you back from this powerful, wholehearted relationship!

Contents

Contents

Preface

*But you are not controlled by your sinful nature. You are controlled by the Spirit if you have the Spirit of God living in you. (And remember that those who do not have **the Spirit of Christ** living in them do not belong to him at all.) **And Christ lives within you**, so even though your body will die because of sin, the Spirit gives you life because you have been made right with God. The Spirit of God, who raised Jesus from the dead, lives in you. And just as God raised Christ Jesus from the dead, he will give life to your mortal bodies by this same Spirit living within you.* Romans 8:9-11

We are going to look at some activities of the greatest life form on the earth today. He is the Holy Spirit who has no body of his own. The Spirit somehow lives in the bodies of people who are born again. Coming down from God and Jesus he is the perfect guide for godly humans. The population of this planet exists solely because God, for his own reasons, decided to create the universe as the place for the history of his new family to take place. The one and only God created us and he loves humans beyond any explanation. The Scripture says: *God decided in advance to adopt us into his own family by bringing us to himself through Jesus Christ. **This is what he wanted to do, and it gave him great pleasure.** So we praise God for the glorious grace he has poured out on us who belong to his dear Son. Ephesians 1:5-6* The Holy Spirit is placed in us because God loves us. People are offered unbelievable opportunities to become a part of the spirit life. God does exist as three individuals working together perfectly (Father, Son, and Holy Spirit.)

This small book is about the many ways that the Scriptures clearly present the power and activity of the Holy Spirit. While studying the Scriptures it becomes obvious that the Spirit is working to make God real to everyone who will have faith in the Gospel message. We want the Spirit in our life but only by obeying God will we have complete victory. The Bible says:... *the Holy Spirit, who is given by God **to those who obey*** *him."* *Acts 5:32b* Chapter One of this paperback is about Jesus to remind us that the Spirit is *always* representing the Savior who is our master. When John looked into the throne room in Heaven he only saw two thrones. The first one belongs to God the Father and the second one belongs to Jesus his Son. There is no throne for the Spirit. However when John looked closely he saw symbols for the Holy Spirit on and around Jesus. All of the symbols were in numbers of seven and we are told they represent the Holy Spirit. This indicates that Jesus and the Spirit of God are coupled closely together.

We may not know how their unity works but it is sacred and it needs our respect. When Jesus was ministering along with his disciples he warned the people that the Holy Spirit was to be honored. Jesus said: *But if I am casting out demons by the Spirit of God, then **the Kingdom of God has arrived among you**. "Anyone who isn't with me opposes me, and anyone who isn't working with me is actually working against me. "Every sin and blasphemy can be forgiven—**except blasphemy against the Holy Spirit**, which will never be forgiven. Anyone who speaks against the Son of Man can be forgiven, but anyone who speaks against the Holy Spirit will never be forgiven, either in this world or in the world to come. Matthew 12:28,30-32* Both saved and unsaved had better be careful what they think and say about the quiet but powerful Spirit. This is not a religious game that we are playing. It is the most important issue in our life.

The Holy Spirit does so much in our life that some people have become focused on him. We must always remember that the three Persons of God are acting together in everything because they are our entire single God. The Lord loves humans an incredible amount and sometimes we may wonder why. We are loved so much that God made us the central reason for all of his creation in this time dimension. It seems odd but making people the central reason for everything in the universe is not popular with worldly people. Instead of gladly receiving the exclusive love of God they would rather chose to believe that they are alive by some kind of a freak accident that brought them into existence. People have a problem with their independence and it is something the Spirit must continually deal with. The Spirit is here on earth to do many works but mainly in a yielded Christian life. This is what it takes to accomplish the will of God. It seems amazing that the Almighty allows humans to do anything in his Kingdom at all.

Of all the wonderful promises that God has given to humans, his Holy Spirit is one of the greatest. The old prophets told Israel that in the last days the Spirit would be poured out. Paul said it was so we could glorify God in the end times: *And now you Gentiles have also heard the truth, the Good News that God saves you. And when you believed in Christ, he identified you as his own by giving you the Holy Spirit, **whom he promised long ago**. Ephesians 1:13* Of course the Spirit has been a gift to people throughout history. When Joseph was in Egypt, the Spirit was there doing his work: *So Pharaoh asked his officials, "Can we find anyone else like this man so obviously **filled with the spirit of God?"** Genesis 41:38* The Spirit may be invisible but his influence is so great that he has caused all the good things in our history. Imagine facing the end of our world without the help of the Holy Spirit. Christians have the privilege of participating as the Spirit fulfills the many good promises that God has made. The Holy Spirit is the power of God and he can accomplish anything.

Eventually when the testing of people has been finished this dimension of time and everything in our universe will be destroyed. It will probably disappear into a black hole. People who insist on clinging to their own style of life will in due course be sent to the Lake of Fire. Humans were created in God's image in order to be capable of entering into a fellowship with him. Our fallen lives must be restored to God's image. His Spirit comes to people daily looking for a repentant soul so God can redeem them and adopt them into his eternal family. The Holy Spirit was given the task of developing God's new family. This is a huge responsibility and the Spirit of God is the only one on Earth who has the power to develop God's righteous family. Born again people have the incredible privilege of being part of God's wonderful eternal future. Hopefully this book will help some people to find their proper place in the family of God.

*For I know that as you pray for me and **the Spirit of Jesus Christ** helps me, this will lead to my deliverance. Philippians 1:19*

Introduction

*Turn you at my reproof: behold, I will **pour out my spirit unto you**, I will make known my words unto you.* Proverbs 1:23 (KJV)

Pouring the Spirit out is conditional. It depends on the FAITH of the servant. To fully know the Holy Spirit it will be necessary to completely accept as true every Word of God. Christians will seek to accept the quiet instructions that guide us through these mighty scriptures. Obeying instructions is difficult for people because humans desire to do things their own way. Somehow we must learn to honor our Almighty God in everything. He is the trusted leader of his Son and the Holy Spirit and having us follow is very important to the Father. Incredibly, the trinity does everything in perfect harmony and we are joining them. Jesus told his disciples that to see and know him on earth was exactly the same as knowing the Father. Our own spirit is actually returning to the image of our God when we live with the power of the Spirit guiding our life. A righteous life is how a human learns to know the Almighty. God pours the same Spirit into each of us so we can have complete unity with Him and others. Our faith is what allows his *Outpouring* of the Spirit into us.

In human history the Father has communicated with people in many ways. The reality of his love for humans can be seen in the complexity and beauty of our universe as well as the earth we live on or the bodies we exist in. But the final word of his love for people is revealed to us by the birth, death, resurrection and ascension of Jesus Christ. Then in order for Jesus to be a reality for us today the Holy Spirit was sent to live in a new way with believers. On the day of Pentecost God gave us the Spirit who works as a team with Jesus. The only way to join the redeemed family of God is to have faith in the plan that Jesus has for each believer. The Spirit, part of the Trinity, is always representing both God and God's Son Jesus. Humans may not be able to prove anything about our infinite God but we can describe him by the attributes we find in the Scriptures and he has many. No one can begin to understand the infinity of God other than through Jesus and the Spirit. These two comforters of humanity can present God the Father to us in wondrous ways. Our Father has made great promises to mankind and he has proved his intention to keep every one of them.

The fantastic grace of God is certainly on full display as we study the works of the Holy Spirit. People of faith will always have the victory because God is continually pouring out his wisdom into every yielded and willing servant. Sadly the church today has missed the power that comes with God's wisdom. This small book is an attempt to wake up the Church to the fact that the power of the Holy Spirit has not been given the attention that is appropriate for this important part of the plan of God. In the old covenant days men struggled to learn Godly wisdom. But today the Lord freely pours out his Spirit into yielded family members. Born again Christians who will continually listen to the Holy Spirit will have an unbelievable life. Because the Spirit is invisible many believers forget how many things he is doing for us. The Holy Spirit was sent by God to live in a saved person so that they can feel and hear the words of God fresh every day. This is the majestic way that God communicates his will for our righteous life.

Although the Spirit is very quiet he has many diverse responsibilities. Hopefully our eyes will open to see how we need to accept all the Spirit's work. We should not worry about what has happened in our past because Jesus is forgiving. Our desire should be to live wholeheartedly for God every day. This is the last days on earth for all born again Christians and we need to serve the Lord like we never have before. God is increasing the outpouring of the Holy Spirit in these last days to combat the flood of evil. Get right with the Savior and be part of a triumphant ending to life. As we enter the last seven years of this civilization the power of the Spirit is available for a victory over every terrible thing that will happen. A Spirit filled person can overcome things that we have never even dreamed of before. The Spirit will testify real hope and comfort to each of us and then enable a clear witness to the people around us. All the wonders of our salvation became real on the day of Pentecost. May we praise our gracious God for allowing us to share in his glory!

*Even as Peter was saying these things, the Holy Spirit fell upon all who were listening to the message. The Jewish believers who came with Peter were amazed that the gift of **the Holy Spirit had been poured out** on the Gentiles, too. For they heard them speaking in tongues and praising God.*
Acts 10:44-46

Chapter One

The Center of Everything

When anyone spends time getting to know the Holy Spirit they must always remember that Jesus Christ is the absolute center hub of everything that transpires between humans and our God. The Father and the Holy Spirit support and rely on the life and death of Jesus in his work to reconcile the human race with our great creator, who is the Trinity itself. Let's be reminded of a few things that God's word says about Jesus our Savior.

*John 3:17 God sent his Son into the world… to save the world **through him**.*

*John 5:23… Anyone who does not **honor the Son** is certainly not honoring the Father who sent him.*

*John 6:54 Anyone who eats my flesh and drinks my blood **has eternal life**, and I will raise that person at the last day.*

*John 11:25… I am the resurrection and the life. Anyone who believes in me will live, **even after dying**.*

*John 20:29… You believe because you have seen me. Blessed are **those who believe without seeing** me.*

Yes, Jesus is the foundation rock of everything in the plan to build a family for God. This wonderful future is available free of cost to every person that will humbly seek Jesus.

The life of simple undivided faith in God is the most wonderful thing that can happen to anyone. It is always available and saved people will be rewarded when they share in the inheritance of Jesus. Our Savior is the person that we imitate as we learn to please God. The Holy Spirit does our uniting to Christ in a silent way that people cannot understand but it is the most real thing in the life of a believer. Here is what Paul said about it: *For you are all children of God through faith in Christ Jesus. And **all who have been united** with Christ in baptism have put on the character of Christ, like putting on new clothes. Galatians 3:26-27* After living in the rags of evil and sin the character of Christ becomes a new suit of righteous. These new clothes reflect the power of our new master who is Jesus. We can now be part of the greatest family ever:... *You are citizens along with all of God's holy people. You are members of God's family. Together, we are his house, built on the foundation of the apostles and the prophets. And **the cornerstone is Christ Jesus** himself. Ephesians 2:20* Jesus is the center but the Spirit is his all powerful partner.

However our Savior has another side to him that the world will soon experience. In the last book of the Bible we are shown a picture of the resurrected Jesus. ***Revelation 1:13-18*** ... *He was wearing a long robe with a gold sash across his chest. His head and his hair were white like wool, as white as snow. And his eyes were like flames of fire. His feet were like polished bronze refined in a furnace, and his voice thundered like mighty ocean waves. He held seven stars in his right hand, and a sharp two-edged sword came from his mouth. And his face was like the sun in all its brilliance. When I saw him, I fell at his feet as if I were dead. But he laid his right hand on me and said, "Don't be afraid! I am the First and the Last. I am the living one. **I died, but look—I am alive forever and ever!** And I hold the keys of death and the grave.* The unsaved world today can only ridicule his bloody human body hanging on the deadly Roman cross. People of faith all know that Jesus actually sacrificed himself for believers and he is worthy to rule as King of everything. Worldly people do not understand the enormous power that the Spirit restored to Jesus after his resurrection.

God's power is in the Holy Spirit. Jesus is alive today because the Spirit supplied the power to raise him out of death. We should learn about the power of the Spirit so we can rise out of our death. Everything we need must draw on his enormous capability. Jesus lived his entire life in this power. Amazingly the power of the Spirit is alive in Christians as we obey Jesus and build our relationship with God. The Scriptures explain how that the wisdom of God teaches us how our new life is empowered: *So we tell others about Christ, warning everyone and **teaching everyone with all the wisdom** God has given us. We want to present them to God, perfect in their relationship to Christ. That's why I work and struggle so hard, depending on **Christ's mighty power that works within me.** Colossians 1:28-29* Real wisdom is accepting our forgiveness of sin by Jesus and the Spirit's power working in us to serve him. On the day of Pentecost the Spirit began to act in the power of the blood of Jesus to accomplish our salvation.

We don't know how the Spirit does his work but the Scriptures tell us unusual things about Heaven. The Bible says: *Jesus had <u>seven horns</u> and <u>seven eyes</u>, which **represent the sevenfold Spirit** of God that is sent out into every part of the earth. Revelation 5:6b* The power of God reaches into the far corners of the earth from God's throne room in Heaven. This is where God's Spirit has his base of operation. Scripture says: *From the throne came flashes of lightning and the rumble of thunder. And in front of the throne were <u>seven torches with burning flames</u>. **This is the sevenfold Spirit of God.** Revelation 4:5* In some powerful way the Son and the Spirit are tied together and we can see their unity in this verse: ***from the sevenfold Spirit** before his throne; **and from Jesus Christ.** Rev. 1:4b* Maybe the seven horns represent **the power** of the Spirit. And it is possible that the seven eyes are the complete **righteous of Jesus** that the Spirit brings into the world. The seven flames might represent **the coming judgment** of the whole world. (Ref. John 16:8) May the Lord help us to accept the unusual way the leadership of Jesus is brought to earth by the Spirit!

Amazingly the Spirit does everything for us pertaining to eternity. Let's look at Galatians which is the first book Paul wrote. This Apostle is the leader in knowledge about the Holy Spirit. Hopefully this book will show us the practical application of the Spirit's work in our life. This means that the Spirit leads believers in everything necessary for their life

_ _ .'ing Jesus. We will learn to know God because the Spirit lives inside of us. Paul was writing this letter to the people he had led to salvation on his first missionary journey. They were confused on exactly how to find the power they needed to live this new covenant life for God. Most of them were Jews and felt that they should continue to follow the Old Testament ways of living. The old way to serve God depended on each person working hard to be good enough for Heaven but no one could live well enough. They had heard the new way of trusting in Christ but were afraid to give their life over to the leading of the Spirit. People would rather do something themselves than simply trust another. They grow up wanting to handle everything their own way.

Paul presented the New Testament Gospel of grace as our only chance to live in Heaven. He knew very well from his personal meeting with the Savior that Jesus along with the Spirit are the only way to God. To direct our way he instructed us to follow the Spirit who has come to live in us. There is no other way to find eternal life except through Jesus and his Spirit. Christians are to communicate with God through the Spirit allowing God to direct our life. The wisdom of God's words can then pass through us to the people around us. Only the Spirit can make the message come alive in the heart of someone. The fact is that many people will not believe that the power of God is able to live inside of a Christian and actually give them super power. Many church people have never even testified or given credit to the Spirit that lives in them. Our new life should be very different than the repetitive religious ways that men have of serving God. The first three chapters of Corinthians explain that men's wisdom in religion is just no good. Pastors are supposed to teach us about the New Testament ways of the Spirit as he works among the people.

Every Christian must learn to follow the Holy Spirit! Believers can then be empowered to live righteously and spread the Gospel message. This is the message: a human will be redeemed if they will humbly repent and live righteously for Jesus. Paul wrote to the Galatians about the new role of the Holy Spirit. Here he asks this question and then answers it. *Let me ask you this one question: Did you receive the Holy Spirit by obeying the Law of Moses? Of course not!* **You received the Spirit because <u>you</u>**

believed the message you heard about Christ. *How foolish can you be? After starting your Christian lives in the Spirit, why are you now trying to become perfect by your own human effort? Galatians 3:2-3* We know that the Old Testament required a lot of human effort and it is difficult for some people to believe that faith in Jesus is enough to please the Almighty. Our genuine faith will include obedience to God.

The idea of working hard to become righteous was ingrained in the Jewish people. Even today people still want to earn merit points by doing certain religious things. Unfortunately the Scriptures say that not even the best human is good enough to live with God. Faith is the most wonderful part of the Gospel message. Paul tells us that every believer will receive the Holy Spirit at the time they are born again. In other words serving Jesus would be impossible except that we have the Spirit who can lead us if we will follow. The Spirit is given to us so that we can be directly connected to Jesus. This allows us to learn the Gospel message firsthand although Jesus returned to Heaven 2000 years ago. The Bible tells us that the Spirit makes us know absolutely if we are saved. This assurance is important because our Christian life is to be lived by believing that anything is possible with God's power. We need to be aware of his hand in our daily life.

Abraham was the first man to whom God gave the promise that faith would save him. Now we can be part of that same promise. Scripture says: *Through Christ Jesus, God has blessed the Gentiles with the same blessing he promised to Abraham, so that we who are believers might* **receive the promised Holy Spirit through faith.** *Galatians 3:14* This gives the Jew and the Gentile the same opportunity for salvation today. Every human is born unrighteous and our religion must be one that leads us into righteousness. This is the only way we will ever live with our righteous Creator. Most people have the bad habit of devising their own way to God. There is no other religion on the face of this earth that has the power to allow a person to meet face to face with God. People must seek Jesus as their Savior, he is the only way to Heaven. Because there is only one way it is very important to get it right.

Jesus is the only way to God and his eternity in Heaven and there are warnings about doing it wrong in the Scriptures. Paul says: *For if you are trying to make yourselves right with God by keeping the law, you have been cut off from Christ! You have fallen away from God's grace. But **we who live by the Spirit** eagerly wait to **receive by faith the righteousness** God has promised to us. Galatians 5:4-5* Thinking we are a good person will separate us from Jesus because we are not a good person when compared with Jesus. Only the Savior is completely good and through the Spirit we must learn to depend on his righteousness. The last verse showed us that only by following the guidance of the Spirit will we ever serve the Savior properly. Of course we do good deeds after salvation but they must be directed by the righteous Holy Spirit. When believers follow the Spirit he will give us the good deeds that are part of God's glory.

The first thing that must happen in the new life is felt by every convert. We instinctively know that we must abandon any worldly ways that we have been enjoying. On the long road of life there is only one successful way to have victory over our old nature. The Bible says: *So I say, **let the Holy Spirit guide your lives**. Then you won't be doing what your sinful nature craves. The sinful nature wants to do evil, which is just the opposite of what the Spirit wants. And **the Spirit gives us desires** that are the opposite of what the sinful nature desires. Galatians 5:16-17a* This is the guidance that will give us success in our quest for righteousness. These wonderful new desires drive out the old nature that have always triggered our failures. Most people have tried and failed to follow some DIY book to break old habits or develop a new one. But the good news is that a born again person will now have the desire to live righteously without working at each small step to good habits. This will bring success and relief to us.

Righteous desires are the guidelines that the Spirit lives by. Paul now explains what to expect from the Spirit when he lives in us. Scripture says: ***The Holy Spirit produces** this kind of fruit in our lives: love, joy, peace, patience, kindness, goodness, faithfulness, gentleness, and self-control. There is no law against these things!* (Because God places these things in our soul we can follow them and find success in righteousness.)

Those who belong to Christ Jesus have nailed the passions and desires of their sinful nature to his cross and crucified them there. Since we are living by the Spirit, **let us follow the Spirit's leading** *in every part of our lives. Galatians 5:22-25* We can easily see how these wonderful characteristics can affect every action that we take in our daily lives. A life of faith means that we can quit trying to earn good points by working ourselves to death. Some people have left the church because of their own hard work.

Paul's explanation of the Gospel to the Galatians is very helpful to people who have made a start with Jesus but their progress as a Christian has slowed or even stopped. The Lord gave us the Spirit so we could mature in righteousness and our progress with God would never stop. We can depend on the Spirit to continually keep our Christian life fresh: *Those who live only to satisfy their own sinful nature will harvest decay and death from that sinful nature. But those who live to please the Spirit* **will** *harvest everlasting life from the Spirit.* **So let's not get tired of doing what is good.** *At just the right time we will reap a harvest of blessing if we don't give up. Galatians 6:8-9* It is now possible to have a continual harvest of good deeds here on earth that will please the Father. Remember our reward is eternal life. The mission of the Holy Spirit is absolutely necessary for our complete salvation. We must have His help.

The Spirit and his relationship with humans is an intriguing story. We are specifically referring to the role of the Spirit that began at Pentecost after Jesus had gone back to Heaven. Every one that Jesus saves will have some kind of relationship with the Spirit. Paul said: *The Good News is about his Son, Jesus. In his earthly life he was born into King David's family line, and he was shown to be the Son of God when he was raised from the dead* **by the power of the Holy Spirit**. *He is Jesus Christ our Lord. Romans 1:3-4* The Spirit empowered the entire life of the Savior and now he will do the same for us. Our saving faith in Jesus includes seeking God forever. This is why the Spirit must direct our life: *He will give eternal life to those who keep on doing good,* **seeking after** *the glory and honor and immortality that God offers. Romans 2:7* Of course the Christian life has many trials but God wants us to see what we are really like and to find out how much we love living with Him.

No matter how difficult our life becomes we can always remember this great truth. Bible says: *Despite all these things, **overwhelming victory is ours** through Christ, who loved us. Romans 8:37* The Spirit is always praying for us. This is real family help that we all need: *And the Father who knows all hearts knows what the Spirit is saying, for the Spirit pleads for us believers **in harmony with God's** own will. Romans 8:27* The beauty of what the Spirit does for us is beyond our description. And God's goodness is not over: *... Even though **we have the Holy Spirit within us as a foretaste** of future glory, we long for our bodies to be released from sin and suffering. We, too, wait with eager hope for the day when God will give us our full rights as his adopted children, including the new bodies he has promised us. Romans 8:23* We have been looking at the central importance of Jesus and the Spirit to our redemption with God. But now let's look at the wide variety of things the Holy Spirit is doing in his mission to build the family of God.

Chapter Two

Building a Family

Jesus sent the Holy Spirit to live in Christians as his comforting representative for the last 2000 thousand years of our history. The Spirit and Jesus are always together in their work but the Holy Spirit is the one that lives in us. His own unusually quiet character is beyond human understanding, but we can learn about the Spirit by the way he has always worked with people. In Revelation 5:6 we can find these intriguing words *"**the seven fold Spirit of God** is sent out into every part of the Earth."* From this verse we understand that the Spirit came to earth long ago with seven major missions to accomplish. The Scripture does not give us the names of the seven. We do know that the Spirit always promotes righteous activities and he comforts the faithful in their times of need. The Spirit has worked faithfully to build a family for God. At times he will measure out judgment to the unrighteous of this earth.

Looking back at Old Testament history we see that the Spirit has always worked to save a people from Satan. At the very beginning of our earth's history the Bible tells us about some of the Spirit's original physical work. *The earth was without form, and void; and darkness was upon the face of the deep. And **the Spirit of God** moved upon the face of the waters. Genesis 1:2 (KJV)* The Holy Spirit did the work to create our home in this universe. We were given the earth where humans could be born and haply live out their lives. Humans don't even know their exact location in the universe but we are born here and it is the place God has prepared for us. It can be a lot of fun to consider the beauty of creation and that we are a part of it. Of course the miraculous wonders performed by the "Spirit of Creation" are incredible and have kept our scientists busy studying for years.

Praise the Lord for the creative works of the Spirit. He is the one who breathes life into every human ever born. The Bible says: *And the LORD God formed man of the dust of the ground, and breathed into his nostrils the breath of life; and* **man became a living soul.** *Genesis 2:7 (KJV)* Creating our original body, mind and the spirit were all done by the Spirit's creative power. But in the spiritual world creation is still taking place today. We should understand that the astounding power of the Spirit can create two different lives for each person today. Our first life is physical but He can give us a second life which is spiritual. We know that on the sixth day of creation the Spirit of God breathed life into the first human being. The Spirit also helps us through our life and will give us a new body after we die. When humans ask Jesus to save them is when the Spirit comes into them to create a new spiritual person.

We are the only creation that has received an eternal spirit which is in the image of God. The original human has been the pattern for the billions of humans reproduced over the years. But because of the "fall" these billions of people are all flawed. But the creative power of God's Spirit that can make us into a new spiritual creature. *The Scriptures tell us, "The first man, Adam, became a living person." But the last Adam—that is, Christ—is a life-giving Spirit. What comes first is the natural body,* **then the spiritual body comes later.** *Adam, the first man, was made from the dust of the earth, while Christ, the second man, came from heaven. 1 Corinthians 15:45-47* Here we see that Christ in us is the "life giving Spirit." How wonderful is it that a precious eternal life is contained in each human. Being made in the actual image of God means we will live forever in Hell or in Heaven. The eternal life of every person is in danger because of disobedience.

Adam was the beginning of the greatest storyline ever imagined and it is all about redemption. The human relationship with God began at a beautiful garden located in the Middle East. This is the place where the invisible Spirit first breathed life into a human and he has continued to do it for each person. But every human has a life or death decision to make about their place in eternity. The Bible says: *So you see, just as death came into the world through a man, now the resurrection from the dead has begun through another man. Just as everyone dies because we all belong to Adam, everyone who belongs to Christ will be given new life. 1 Corinthians 15:21-22* We must believe that the Spirit is the power of the Almighty for every work in our redemption by the blood of Christ.

In the original garden Adam had the astonishing experience of physically walking with God. That relationship with God was taken away when the first two people disobeyed. Adam was the only human to have the privilege of physically walking with God. His disobedience is the reason God put into action his seven thousand year plan to save repentant humans and have them become his family. Christians will soon have the privilege of living with God in eternity. Of Course we understand that the redemption plan that gives us a relationship with God is all centered around Jesus who died on the cruel cross. Jesus is in Heaven today and the Spirit is the one on earth who breathes spiritual life into each new Christian. The Bible tells us about the salvation plan that we all follow: *Jesus replied, "I assure you, no one can enter the Kingdom of God without being born of water* (first) *and the Spirit* (second). *John 3:5* Every Christian must learn to live by their faith in the power and reality of the living Jesus Christ.

Today the power of the Spirit to *create* is still at work on earth. It is controversial of course but the Spirit uses his power to create even more than a born again soul. Just like the days when Jesus was on the earth the Spirit can heal people for the purposes of God. The most noticeable signs of the Spirit's power are the times when a dead person is raised to life. Not even death can resist the power of the Spirit when it is God's will. Look what Jesus said about the power in this verse. *Is it easier to say 'Your sins are forgiven,' or 'Stand up and walk'? Luke 5:23* It is plain to see here that the Spirit of Jesus can just as easily supply spiritual life or physical life from the same power. God is the only creator of life and people's small thinking does not change a thing. Even the innovative powers of people were given as a gift and should be used righteously.

God tells us that the creation of humans was a totally successful mission. But then a terrible thing happened when Adam and Eve decided not to obey God's directions. Every person on earth was doomed because we are born into Adam's family of sinners. The perfect Garden of Eden had to be closed and the people went out to live in the cursed world. Because of sin humans then became worse and worse until everyone on Earth had to be destroyed. The Spirit then made a change to human lives. God saw that man was living to long and his lifetime needed to be shortened: *Genesis 6:3 Then the LORD said, "My Spirit will not put up with humans for such a long time, **for they are only mortal flesh.** ...* So the flood was sent to wipe out all these original evil people. However one family of eight was saved in the Ark, to restart our world once again.

Another important mission of the Holy Spirit was to create the nation of Israel. God asked Abram to leave his home and move his family all the way to the sinful land of Canaan. Abram was born 2000 years after the creation of man and God wanted a people of faith in him. However it was another 430 years before the Jewish slaves were allowed to enter Canaan and receive the promises of a new people and a new land. But the Spirit is always continuing his mission to build a family for God. We can read about how the righteousness of God was at work: *Genesis 41:37 Joseph's suggestions were well received by Pharaoh and his officials. So Pharaoh asked his officials, "Can we find anyone else like this man so obviously **filled with the spirit of God?** "* It seems here that God has always been known even by people who don't serve him.

Moses, the old covenant law giver and leader of the new nation of Israel, was certainly a great mission of the Spirit. He was protected as a child in the house of the enemy Pharaoh. Then the Spirit led him to safety in the desert for 40 years. At the right time Moses was instructed to stand up for the slave nation and demand their freedom. The Spirit certainly had a job convincing Pharaoh but when the angel of death passed through Egypt the king decided to let the Israelites go. Then Pharaoh, changing his mind, chased the slave nation up against the mighty Red Sea but the Spirit guarded them with fire and opened-up a nine mile dry road through the middle of all its water. The sea saved Israel but that same day it closed and killed the army of Egypt. The Spirit even made the all the shoes of the Israelites last for forty years in the wilderness of Arabia. It is interesting that every time Moses went into the tabernacle to receive more of the Law, upon leaving he had to cover his face because the people could not stand the glow of the Holy Spirit until it had worn off.

Another great story of the Spirit's missions during the Old Testament time was David. This highly favored man of God and was blessed with a leading role as the King of God's chosen people. He also became the great grandfather of Jesus, the Savior of the world. The Spirit came over David many times. Sometimes the Spirit saved him in battles and sometimes he inspired him with great Psalms of praise. David was so in love with God that he one time asked if God was so good to anybody else in the world. We may not have the same worldly blessing down here but we all have the opportunity of being blessed even more in our eternal life. The Spirit of God worked continually with the people of Israel trying to separate them from idols. Unfortunately, the promises made to Abraham as well as the Law that was written down by Moses were ignored most of the time. There was certainly a need for the better Covenant that was later given one that did not depend on the works of people. The new covenant is available for us today.

Remember that the Holy Spirit came over people in the Old Testament and their deeds were very noticeable. But the Spirit did not live inside of people to have the personal relationship that a Christian has available today. This could only happen after Jesus was gone back to Heaven. The Scripture says: *But you will receive power when the Holy Spirit comes upon you. And you will be my witnesses, telling people about me everywhere—in Jerusalem, throughout Judea, in Samaria, and to the ends of the earth." Acts 1:8* As much as the saints of old wanted this powerful help, the new covenant relationship was not possible until the Day of Pentecost. The Savior had lived 33 years of perfect life before becoming the sacrifice for the original sin of mankind. After Jesus had finished his redemption work he returned to God and they sent the Spirit to help New Testament believers live a new and victorious life. We will see how this happens in further chapters.

Chapter Three

Two Worlds for Humans

Physical missions of building our universe and then guiding the history of mankind are not the complete sevenfold work that God gave the Spirit. It could be that all this tremendous physical work was counted only as one of the seven-fold missions. We know that the Holy Spirit is living in at least two realms which are both the physical and spiritual worlds. It is certain that he was given missions in both of these worlds. These are different types of missions because one is about the eternal home of God and the other is simply our temporary universe that God has provided for our creation and development. The eternal life of a born again person is all about returning to the righteousness that we were intended to have. The fact is that humans don't naturally want to live righteously today because of our sin. The process of redeeming people is done individually and only a small percentage of the population will ever become part of God's eternal family. Let's look at some of the many spiritual tasks that the Spirit is accomplishing while guiding our redemption path into the spiritual world.

The spiritual purpose of humans is to honor God. This began the day Adam was created and has never ended. The creation of the human family will always be for the great purpose of God's glory. A loving family is something that God really wants. People were originally created in a righteous relationship with the Creator. But after we rebelled God needed a family that chose him out of love. If he, in some way, forced everybody to love him it would not create the kind of eternal family that he desires. We have the opportunity to be the kind of person that he wants when we humble ourselves. Satan developed a hatred for God at some point in the past. He jealously wants humans to worship him in his many evil ways. Ever since Adam decided not to obey God the Devil has tempted everyone hoping they will follow him into evil pleasures. This greatly increased the work of the Holy Spirit, who is the power of God, wanting to redeem us and make us capable of a relationship with God. This is what we were intended for originally.

The Bible says that the power needed for the completion of the redemption plan (the blood of Jesus) was sent to us at just the right time in history. It happened 4000 years after the creation of Adam when the Savior came physically into our world. This was the power needed to complete God's redemption plan and we are privileged to seek a place in God's family. There is a place prepared for repentant people. The Spirit was always with Jesus but he became very noticeable when he united with Jesus for their ministry of grace in these last days. We are told by God: *Luke 3:21-23 One day when the crowds were being baptized, Jesus himself was baptized. As he was praying, the heavens opened, **and the Holy Spirit, in bodily form**, descended on him like a dove. And a voice from heaven said, "You are my dearly loved Son, and you bring me great joy."* The Spirit was very active in the life of Jesus and his disciples. Satan had Jesus killed thinking that would give him victory. However, Jesus overcame all evil by sacrificing himself and becoming victorious over every obstacle that would prevent our salvation.

It was a wonderful Pentecost day that came soon after Jesus had ascended to Heaven. The Spirit came to live in the first 120 people and then the Spirit quickly added another 3000 souls. *Acts 2:1-4 On the day of Pentecost all the believers were meeting together in one place. Suddenly, there was a sound from heaven like the roaring of a mighty windstorm, and it filled the house where they were sitting. Then, what looked like flames or tongues of fire appeared and settled on each of them. And everyone present was filled with the Holy Spirit and began speaking in other languages, as the Holy Spirit gave them this ability.* Peter, compelled by the Holy Spirit, stepped forward and preached his first Spirit filled sermon about what had just happened. Since that time we are aware that because of the sin in people the 2000 years of church history have gone up and down in spirituality. But the Holy Spirit has endured every bit of it while living in Christians and quietly doing his work. The light has never gone completely out in this world. The Spirit does not force anybody but always continues his work. The church today should celebrate every Pentecost the way that Paul did every year.

Paul spent his life teaching people about the revelation of truth that Jesus and the Spirit of God have made available to everyone. By the grace of God, both Jesus and the Spirit came to earth with the purpose of rescuing the fallen and doomed creation of human beings. They are continually bringing the truth and a lot of much needed revelation to the born again people. None of us deserve to be saved and taken to live with God. Paul said: *And because it is through God's kindness, then it is not by our good works. For in that case, God's **grace** would not be what it really is—free and undeserved. Romans 11:6* We should recognize how much we need the love of God every day. Every born again believer has the privilege of the spirit of revelation living in them. A Christian will have something revealed to them every time they seek the Lord. Some servants of God have had thousands of revelations given to them and they have just begun to learn the truth of God. When we are devoted to our Creator he will teach us truth so we can recognize the enemy to our righteous life.

Jesus spent three years teaching his disciples every day. This is almost enough time to receive a college degree but it was not enough. Before leaving earth Jesus promised another comforter would take his place and represent him. Here is part of his introduction: *He is the Holy Spirit, who leads into **all truth**. The world cannot receive him, because it isn't looking for him and doesn't recognize him. But you know him, because he lives with you now and later will be in you. John 14:17* Jesus informs them that the Spirit will have the ability to reveal many supernatural things to them. Some believers feel that we can learn everything we need to know from the Bible. In my Spirit led experience, the Lord has helped me in situations that are not written in the Scriptures. There are occasions when at a later time the Spirit will show me the same basic truth from the Bible. It is very reassuring to know the Lord is working in many different ways.

The fact is that some believers in today's world don't have a Bible but the Lord is still teaching them his truth every day. Revelation from the Spirit is necessary for salvation and all other spiritual mysteries. For example things like love are not easily taught only by a book. We know that experience will teach us much more. Scholars mistakenly think they can understand the mysteries of God by using their logic. But Paul tells us plainly where the truth is hidden: *I want them to be encouraged and knit together by strong ties of love. I want them to have complete confidence that they understand God's mysterious plan, which is Christ himself. In him lie hidden all the treasures of wisdom and knowledge. Colossians 2:2-3* If the Spirit of Jesus does not reveal the truth then we will never find the saving truth. The very word revelation means the disclosure of something we do not know. We must rely on the Spirit to teach us truth.

Even cleanliness is connected to the subject of revelation. God must show each of us how that our unclean life has separated us from Him. The Spirit will put great effort into revealing how to live a godly life in our old fallen body. Holiness is required by God. We have all heard about Christians who have allowed sin to ruin their righteous life. If they could tell us the truth it would be a warning about how miserable their life had become because of their sin. A good relationship with God is certainly worth living a clean life. The Scripture explains: *Because we have these promises,* (the truth) *dear friends, let us cleanse ourselves from everything that can defile our body or spirit. And let us work toward complete holiness because we fear God. 2 Corinthians 7:1* Staying clean is something that we are responsible for. The Spirit does tell us when we are wrong but it is much easier being holy when we stay busy serving the Lord. Jesus told Peter that he was clean all over but that he must still wash his hands and feet. This applies to believers today.

Here is the spiritual reason given by Jesus: *You have already been pruned and purified by the message I have given you. John 15:3* When the Gospel message is revealed to us, the forgiveness of Jesus will cleanse our life for eternity. However we do sin occasionally in our Christian life and that is something we must certainly address. John said: *But if we confess our sins to him, he is faithful and just to forgive us our sins and to cleanse us from all wickedness. 1 John 1:9* This is the washing of our hands and feet. In his great grace the Lord will forgive his children again and again. Some people call 1 John 1:9 the Christian bar of soap. There are people who think they can use this as a way to cheat their way into Heaven. They will absolutely fail because God knows the motive in every heart. The Spirit wants to help everyone who is serious about serving God. In Romans eight the Bible says that without the Spirit no one will ever go to be with Jesus.

There is great unity found within the revelation of truth that we have in the Spirit. Among humans, unity is a miracle. Knowing the Spirit is the invisible but reliable leader of every Christian we can safely trust his absolute leadership with our life. It is because we have the Spirit of Jesus in our heart that we are allowed to be joined with God and this automatically joins us to other believers. In the big picture when we allow the Spirit to control our life he can place us along with others as a stone in God's eternal Temple. The New Testament says: *And you are living stones that God is building into his spiritual temple. What's more, you are his holy priests. Through the mediation of Jesus Christ, you offer spiritual sacrifices that please God. 1 Peter 2:5* The invisible leader of all the followers of Jesus is today continually expanding the work of Jesus. We should feel this unity much more as the return of Jesus grows close. Unity has been a long and difficult job because the Devil is continually attempting to disrupt the work of God.

Starting with the apostolic days and continuing on through many dark and rough times the invisible Spirit living in the church has made progress with righteous living. Our world has been changed by the many spiritual victories of Christians that have overcome this world. Years ago America was founded on righteousness. The Father sent the Spirit of his son into our heart to change us into a member that is joined in unity. Our union with the Spirit makes us into a new person. The church has been given leaders who remind us of the proper behavior for Christian believers. Paul tells us: *Now these are the gifts Christ gave to the church: the apostles, the prophets, the evangelists, and the pastors and teachers.* **Their responsibility is to equip** *God's people to do his work* **and build up** *the church, the body of Christ. Ephesians 4:11-12* These five types of church leaders must follow the Spirit or the people will suffer spiritual loss.

The facts are that God's grace is Jesus and God's power is the Spirit. We all know that Jesus has a birthday on this earth but so does the Holy Spirit. The Spirit's birthday of living on this earth is the day of Pentecost. Jesus mentioned it during his ministry: *(When Jesus said "living water," he was speaking of the Spirit, who would be given to everyone believing in him. But **the Spirit had not yet been given**, because Jesus had not yet entered into his glory.) John 7:39* The Spirit's first church body was the 120 people on which the flame of the Spirit rested in the upper room. The unity of the original church was so great that rich people were selling properties and giving the money to the poor Christian brothers. Think about the wonderful results that the Holy Spirit and the church have produced by spreading the Gospel for the last 2000 years. At Pentecost God came into this world in a new way and some people will never be the same.

This new anointed church had the privilege of being the first of many people who were bound for Heaven. It was as if 120 trumpeters had gathered to make the announcement that would soon be heard around the world. A brand new kind of invisible power had arrived and he could cause unity among millions of Christians who live on earth today. The Bible says we are one: *Some of us are Jews, some are Gentiles, some are slaves, and some are free. But we have all been baptized into one body by one Spirit, and **we all share the same Spirit**. 1 Corinthians 12:13* This power of unity has been at work in Christian people since the church began. The Acts of the Holy Spirit are recorded in the Scriptures to show the foundations of the wonderful family of God. Jesus gave us the Spirit and everything needed for the victory of the church over this world. Every gift that we receive has the purpose of building his family. If we look at church problems they always begin with a person exercising their self-will instead of seeking the Spirit's guidance.

The power of truth and the unity of the Spirit living in us will bring great comfort in to our life here on earth. This comfort may be much more important than we might think. Living as a Christian in this pagan world would be impossible without this operation of the Spirit. The new life is about righteous living and this world of evil is continually offensive to us. Remember one of the last things Jesus promised his followers before he left earth. *I am leaving you with a gift—peace of mind and heart. And the peace I give **is a gift** the world cannot give. So don't be troubled or afraid. John 14:27* Jesus was talking about the Spirit of comfort bringing peace to the human heart when it is born again. One example is unsaved people who at times are terrified by thoughts of their death. This does not happen to a born again person because we are looking forward to the day we will be with Jesus. This freedom from fear is something very helpful to a life of righteous victories. Peaceful lives are more valuable than a healthy life.

Comfort and peace are also necessary when witnessing to others. Jesus and the disciples would get people's attention with miracles. Although there are miracles today they are not accepted as true by the reasonable "thinkers." However the peace and comfort in our daily life will many times get the attention of the worldly. People are watching to see if we are living the righteous life we are telling them about. The Spirit puts quietness in our mind that is a witness to others of our faith in the Savior. Our invisible faith actually has a lot of substance that cannot be measured. It is kind of like trying to describe how much love we have in our heart. Paul said: *And this hope will not lead to disappointment. For we know how dearly **God loves us**, because he has given us the Holy Spirit to fill our hearts with his love. Romans 5:5* The Spirit of Jesus lives in a redeemed person and our Savior is the essence of God. The love of God is the reason the Spirit gives us comfort and peace.

Peace and comfort contribute to our inner tranquility. Most people in this liberal world are worried and nervous. This is our opportunity to introduce them to the peace and comfort that salvation brings into the faithful. The Spirit brings the love of God into us at our salvation. Everything about the Gospel Message will bring quietness into our soul.

For example, we can contemplate the soon return of our Savior and a wave of calm will sweep over us. When we are talking to an unsaved person they can actually feel the calmness that is in our soul. Our faith in God places us in a position to enjoy the perfect relationship of the Trinity. Because there is no strife within God joining his family gives us access to his privileged relationship. In other words born again people are living in a very peaceful spiritual atmosphere. It is only when we seek the Savior that we can find the comfort of his Spirit.

In the Old Testament days people did not have the Spirit living in them and this same comfort was not available to them. Today the peace that Jesus left with his followers can be a very wonderful part of our lives. Just like everything we enjoy by faith we must accept this truth into our thinking and let it change our behavior. There is no way we can change our natural behavior by doing it ourselves. We change because the Holy Spirit is continually working to make us righteous. Consider this: *And the Holy Spirit helps us **in our weakness**. For example, we don't know what God wants us to pray for. But the Holy Spirit prays for us with groanings that cannot be expressed in words. Romans 8:26* The Word of God and the Spirit are continually encouraging us to fully participate as a sincere member of God's family. Christians have a supernatural peace and comfort available to them.

As we study all that the Spirit does we remember that he was promised by God through the prophets of old. Sometimes we wonder how much these godly men understood what was being promised. Paul said: *And when you believed in Christ, he identified you as his own by giving you the Holy Spirit, **whom he promised long ago.** The Spirit is God's guarantee that **he will give us the inheritance he promised** and that he has purchased us to be his own people. He did this so we would praise and glorify him. Ephesians 1:13b-14* God promised from the beginning a new Spirit to all the repentant people who want to live a godly life. The Scriptures say: *And **I will give you a new heart, and I will put a new spirit in you.** I will take out your stony, stubborn heart and give you a tender, responsive heart. And I will put my Spirit in you so that you will follow my decrees and be careful to obey my regulations. Ezekiel 36:26-27*

To reach heaven, any human being must have the long promised Spirit of God living in them.

King David said: ***Give me understanding*** *and I will obey your instructions;* ***I will put them into practice with all my heart.*** *Make me walk along the path of your commands, for that is where my happiness is found. Psalm 119:34-35* We know that no one could follow all the instructions of God with their own natural powers. Even back then David was asking for the help of the Holy Spirit to live a godly life. We see that in the New Testament Paul brought all people together in the Spirit. *It doesn't matter whether we have been circumcised or not. What counts is whether* ***we have been transformed into a new creation.*** *May God's peace and mercy be upon all who live by this principle; they are the new people of God. Galatians 6:15-16* Living as a righteous person is a place where we can really tie the Old and the New Testament together. We are talking about the life of anyone who believes God's promises and is continually trying to please God with their life.

Our confidence and hope is founded in our Savior. The Scripture says: *For all of God's promises* ***have been fulfilled in Christ*** *with a resounding "Yes!" And through Christ, our "Amen" (which means "Yes") ascends to God for his glory. It is God who enables us, along with you, to stand firm for Christ. He has commissioned us, and he has identified us as his own* ***by placing the Holy Spirit in our hearts*** *as the first installment that guarantees everything he has promised us. 2 Corinthians 1:20-22* It is easy to see here that both Jesus and the Spirit are working toward our redemption. Paul said in another place: *Remember that Christ came as a servant to the Jews to show that* ***God is true to the promises he made*** *to their ancestors. He also came so that the Gentiles might give glory to God for his mercies to them. Romans 15:8-9a* God has put everything out front for Christians and it is hard to believe that some people walk away from him when they become discouraged.

Within the next seven years the world will see the return of Jesus with his justice as well as his tremendous saving power for Israel. Check out these Bible verses: *When I bring them home from the lands of their enemies,* ***I will display my holiness*** *(* Spirit *) among them for all the* *nations to see. Ezekiel 39:27* The whole evil world will get a chance to see godliness in action. The anti-christ will kill two thirds of today's Jews but the good ones will be called: *When I whistle to them, they will come running, **for I have redeemed them.** From the few who are left, they will grow as numerous as they were before. Zechariah 10:8* Israel has waited a long time for this restoration: *I will bring that group through the fire and make them pure. I will refine them like silver and purify them like gold. They will call on my name, and I will answer them. I will say, 'These are my people,' and they will say, 'The LORD is our God.' Zechariah 13:9*

The New Testament confirms this: *And so all Israel will be saved. As the Scriptures say, "The one who rescues will come from Jerusalem, and he will turn Israel away from ungodliness. And this is my covenant with them, that **I will take away their sins.**" Romans 11:26-27* There are two worlds that we are involved with and the spiritual world is far greater than this physical one we are created on. This is why Christians are so heavenly minded that the world has very little use for us. People of this world have no idea how important we are to them. Everything that the Spirit does in either world is for the benefit of the righteous. Do not give up the good fight of faith for it is about to lead us into the greatest eternal life possible. *For we are God's masterpiece. He has created us anew in Christ Jesus, so we can **do the good things he planned for us long ago.** Ephesians 2:10*

Chapter Four

The Chosen

The day of Pentecost was an enormous change in God's plan to redeem humans. People had always been required to clean their lives up and live righteously with human power. It just was not possible. The most wonderful thing happened on the day when the Spirit of Jesus came to live inside of Christians. We needed God's power to clean up our life. Today we have everything needed to please God. Our lives will change when we accept the responsibilities of our adoption. It is wonderful to be a fully accepted member of God's powerful family. Paul even reassures us that we can make it to the last day of our complete salvation: *And I am certain that God, who began the good work within you, will continue his work until it is finally finished on the day when Christ Jesus returns. Philippians 1:6* When we accept that the Spirit can make everything possible in the spiritual world our life will dramatically change. Usually a crisis will come into the life of a believer and they will need extra power to survive as a Christian. We quickly learn that by denying ourselves of this world and yielding our life completely to God will bring unbelievable solutions for us. Our life going forward we long for the power of the Spirit.

Let's consider the necessity for the Spirit of Adoption, which is a precious and lengthy work of the Spirit. The fall of man requires the far reaching plan of redemption in order to save us from our ending in Hell which we all deserve. Sometimes adoption is a lengthy process because the Spirit must work individually with each of us throughout our lifetime. Because of the rebellious fall of humans the Spirit must now lead us through many steps of faith. He does many different things to us while creating our new life with God. All this is required to rebuild our holy walk with God which has always been his purpose. Human rebellion still lives in people today but God's plan of adoption can help us overcome it. Scripture says: *You received God's Spirit when he adopted you as his own children. Now we call him, "Abba, Father." Romans 8:15* The Spirit provides the power to overcome our natural life which can allow us to pursue our desire to walk with the Almighty.

Everybody who lives with God must be righteous. If any unrighteous person were able to gain a presence with God they would immediately die. The Bible says it this way: *Dear children, don't let anyone deceive you about this: When people do what is right, it shows that they are righteous, **even as Christ is righteous**.* (Jesus is the only way to the Father)... *Those who have been born into God's family do not make a practice of sinning, because God's life is in them. So they can't keep on sinning, because they are children of God. ... Anyone who does not live righteously and does not love other believers **does not belong to God***. *1 John 3:7-10* When evil impulses assault us remember that "evil" spelled backwards is 'live." We know that Jesus is always righteous and back in verse two John says "we know that we will be like him." What a wonderful thought for a mortal to realize that in eternity we can be righteous just like Jesus. God designed this privileged position as the goal of our redemption.

The first thing about adoption is that a child does not have the power to adopt a family. Adoption must be brought about by the Father of a family. This must be done properly or there will be no inheritance for the child. Our legal adoption was made possible when Jesus returned to Heaven as Savior and sent the Holy Spirit to earth at Pentecost. The Word of God gives us many beautiful ideas and one of the most loving ones was given by Jesus one day after saving a soul. He said: *"For the Son of Man came **to seek and save** those who are lost." Luke 19:10* This wonderful truth is the beginning of every saved person's new life with God. In other words the Spirit of Jesus is searching the world looking for people the Father wants to adopt into his family. The Father's redemption plan had to wait 4000 yrs for Jesus to arrive on earth and make himself the sacrifice for our sins.

We do have a part to play in choosing our righteous future. It is our faith that God wants from us. Paul said this in a letter: *As for us, we can't help but thank God for you, dear brothers and sisters loved by the Lord. We are always thankful that God chose you to be among the first to experience salvation—a **salvation that came through the Spirit** who makes you holy **and through your belief** (faith) **in the truth.** 2 Thessalonians 2:13* It's very clear that the Spirit is bringing the righteous of Jesus into our life to complete our salvation. At the same time we must live in the faith we receive from the word of God. We believe in the truth of the Bible and live our whole life in this faith. The complete Godhead is working together to make our salvation possible. But in the last verse we see that it is our faith and the power of the Spirit that God requires throughout our life. There is no salvation for people who are not interested in having a faith that is willing to trust in everything God has for them.

Christians should be aware what an enormous job was begun when the Spirit of Adoption moved into our heart. We must learn that our new life will be the result of following the Spirit. Paul tells us many things about the Spirit but here is one of the most powerful: *The Spirit of God, who raised Jesus from the dead, **lives in you.** Romans 8:11a* This is the indwelling of the Holy Spirit and is something we must accept by faith. There is no way that any human can live the holy life without the power of the Spirit in us. Paul said: *So I say, let the Holy Spirit **guide your lives.** Then you won't be doing what your sinful nature craves. Galatians 5:16* While we are living on this earth our old nature will continually tempt us to do wrong by giving in to our selfish desires. However the Spirit living in us is stronger than any desire and our victory is in following his directions. This supernatural power is what allows us to find our eternal freedom.

Have you ever thought how great it would be to have the world's wisest person to advise you in your everyday life? Well that would be nothing compared to having the Spirit of God advising us on what to do at every minute of the day. It's easy for Him because everything in our spirit is well known to him. After our adoption the Spirit is continually in us. Here is what the Bible says: *It was to us that God revealed* (many great) *things by his Spirit. For his Spirit searches out everything and **shows us** God's deep secrets. 1 Corinthians 2:10* Not only does the Spirit know the actual us but we are given the privilege of getting to know the true God. A real servant of God has learned many spiritual mysteries that the worldly person will never know or understand. Over the years of serving Jesus the Holy Spirit will teach us more and more about God's ways. Being a Christian is the most privileged life ever made possible for any creation.

After our spiritual adoption the Spirit begins a transformation of the old nature into a brand new godly nature. He does this by changing our craving for worldly things into devotion to God. For example we don't start our day with some drug that gives us an altered life. Or a believer must deny the urge to be something in front of other believers which is also an altered life. We will desire to read and pray to humbly serve God for that day. Because of this new attitude we begin to be a totally different person. The Scripture says it like this: *This means that anyone who belongs to Christ has become a new person. The old life is gone; **a new life** has begun! 2 Corinthians 5:17* The Spirit of Adoption will change us so that we can live forever with our loving and righteous Savior. When the big Spirit of God joins with our little spirit the result is our new spiritual life. This is the process that rescues people from "the fall" and returns them to the image of God. Our hope of walking with God now becomes a reality.

Our complete adoption is accomplished by the power of the Holy Spirit. From beginning to end Jesus uses the Spirit's power. The Bible says: *He will take our weak mortal bodies and change them into glorious bodies like his own, **using the same power** with which he will bring everything under his control. Philippians 3:21* Any day now the Spirit will remove Christians to another world and he will refocus on subjecting this entire world to the rule of Jesus. But the subject of adoption is straight forward. All Christians are brought into the Spirit of Jesus to form a righteous body here on earth. We read these words: *Make every effort to keep yourselves united in the Spirit, binding yourselves together with peace. For **there is one body and one Spirit**, just as you have been called to one glorious hope for the future. Ephesians 4:3-4* Someday soon the power of the Spirit living in us will take us to meet Jesus. Paul wanted us to find comfort in this meeting: *Then, together with them, we who are still alive and remain on the earth* **will be caught up in the clouds** *to meet the Lord in the air. Then we will be with the Lord forever. 1 Thessalonians 4:17* We are not orphans in this world. Jesus has done everything for our adoption into God's family.

Adoption is much more than legality with God. He is changing his own eternal life by joining his Spirit to ours for eternity and giving us an inheritance to a life we cannot imagine. Because God is a Spirit we even have a difficult time understanding how he has become the main part of our life. However the facts are given to us: *No, I will not abandon you as orphans—I will come to you. ... When I am raised to life again, you will know that I am in my Father, and* **you are in me, and I am in you.** *John 14:18-20* When we read this passage we must think of it spiritually or it will be confusing. The only way Jesus is in us and we are in him must be done by the Holy Spirit of Adoption. We might say that the rich full Spirit comes into our small dried up spirit and fills it up with the life of Jesus. It is then that we have the privilege of allowing the stream of living water to flow out to the people around us.

Children of God have more things to thank God for than we can ever remember. The Spirit has actually adopted us into God's family and each child has a great inheritance. Yes, each Christian will suffer for a while. This is because our complete faith in Christ has made us like Him. But being like Jesus we have become an heir of the promise of faith made to Abraham. This promise says we have eternal life through faith. Anybody becoming God's heir is also guaranteed to have his great counsel in everything. Our hope is solid because we have the right to approach God any time we need or want him. Usually people who have very little in this world will love God quicker and deeper than the wealthy. Therefore most of God's family on earth is poor but their faith is great. The servants of Jesus will someday inherit the eternal kingdom that every Christian is waiting to see. (Ref. Romans 8:15, Galatians 3:27, Titus 3:7, Hebrews 6:17, James 2:5)

Christians need never worry about their life in Heaven because the Spirit in us is continually teaching and directing us how to live a righteous life. The Spirit is the built-in guarantee of our inheritance that God has given to his family. Paul tells the church: *The Spirit is God's guarantee that he will give us the inheritance he promised and that **he has purchased us** to be his own people. He did this so we would praise and glorify him. Ephesians 1:*14 Every day we are following the guidance of the Holy Spirit until the last breath of our life. On that last day of our earthly life the Spirit will simply go with us from this physical world over into the spiritual world. The Spirit of Adoption is working to bring God's human family into a place where the Savior can proudly present them to the Almighty. Every Christian will be completely fulfilled by the eternal life that Jesus has provided. It will be easy to glorify our God.

Chapter Five

God's Will Fulfilled

The world church relies on the Spirit in the same way an individual must do. If the Spirit leads the church of one nation into a revival it is our duty to join in and support the movement. Through prayer and the leading of God's Spirit, Christians help bring unity to historical movements that revive the church. Unity among believers is very important in these days of tribulation. Everything in a Christian life is getting more difficult as Satan tears our world to pieces. Looking back in history we can see how failure to follow the Holy Spirit has deadly results. During the twelve hundred years after Pentecost, the Catholic Church leaders abandoned the Spirit and they took over control of the church. The more those religious men controlled the church the further away from God the church became. Eventually the evil nature of men made the church into the most wicked and immoral force on the earth. The result of this disobedience to God brought the world into a horrible condition that history has called "The dark age of man." People were ravaged by diseases and famines with only a small ray of light maintained.

But then God's Holy Spirit miraculously began to move in a man here and a man there. It took years but the western world changed. The reform of God's church rested on the Spirit moving flawed but vigorous men of God. John Wycliffe and his people in the 1300's began to let the light of God shine in the world. A man named Jan Huss in the 1400's along with the famous Martin Luther worked hard to enliven the Word of God. In the 1500's great men like John Calvin and John Knox spent their lives teaching the lost world. During this time the Spirit united many believers in the rediscovered Word of God that was beginning to be printed for the people. The godly freedom that was reborn completely changed the western world. In the 1600's the Spirit led many believers to leave Europe and build a brand new nation in the West. In the 1900's the Spirit directed the United States to restore the nation of Israel so God could fulfill all the promises he had given to his people.

Christians have now had a 2000 year time of grace and it is our privilege to live at the ending of this special time. In these last days of our age, Christians must watch closely for the movements of the Spirit and support the world wide church. As we support the things that God is doing in the world today every local church must pray that we find the will of God. We must take action today because our days here are short. Don't hold back anything for there is no tomorrow. Soon the seven year tribulation will be over and Jesus along with the Jews will be the last kingdom to rule this earth. The Spirit is directing both individuals and the nations of the world. God has never changed any of his plans for the church or this world. Christians are to support what God is doing because he is perfect. Today we see the end of the Christian World coming near and the Spirit is an absolute necessity to resist Satan's bid to rule over the church.

In order to really understand the importance of the Holy Spirit to believers we should acknowledge the great difference between the Old and New Covenants. The Old Covenant was conditional and required a mutual agreement between parties. This means that the people had agreed to live a good life to receive rewards and had agreed that a bad life would bring punishment. In fact some good people complained that the bad people were not receiving the punishment they deserved. We don't need to list all of people's failures with the Old Covenant because they are well documented in the Word. Obviously it was necessary for a New Covenant to straighten out the mess we were in when Jesus came. Whichever Covenant people are under every human will face judgment at the end of life.

God's New Covenant is completely different than the Old. Instead of the Law we have the promise made to Abraham based on his faith in God. Abraham's promise has no legal requirements to be met by the believing recipient. This is the eternal pledge we can obtain simply by our faith in Jesus. However the success of our righteous life is based on the help of God's Spirit with our life. There is no other way to please our heavenly Father who will give us an unbelievable eternity. Jesus came to earth as the author of the new covenant although he has returned to his honored place in Heaven. He is always concerned with our spiritual condition and said this before leaving: ***Righteousness is available*** *because I go to the Father, and you will see me no more. John 16:10* God then sent the Spirit to live in his children to prompt us in our righteousness.

Sadly, rather than follow our guiding Spirit some believers are actually working against God by trying to control things themselves. We should always be ambassadors for this wonderful Covenant of grace and warn people to listen to the Spirit. Christians today should not be known as people who live by religious rules. We should be known as people who love others because Jesus has forgiven us. The Spirit is patiently teaching God's children how to live in the New Covenant. After salvation we need to eagerly learn how our new life will be completely different than the old. At first new Christians don't know what has changed or how different their life will be. By completely yielding to Jesus a new Christian will learn very quickly. Of course God is the one who ultimately controls everything but he has granted a special freedom in order to show us what kind of people we are.

The Christian life has God as the instructor who teaches his willing students. Christians cannot expect the instructor to do our homework. Today we have many believers who are lazy and are not serious about working to change their life. Because the Holy Spirit is perfect we should remember that any failings in our Christian life are completely our fault and we will be held responsible. God's Spirit is perfect in every way and we must follow him as closely as we possibly can. What will it take to wake up the people in church pews who are asleep and impress them of the potential that waits inside a humble yielded Christian? It is sometimes difficult to accept the grace that God is giving to us. Because of pride some people have made up silly requirements for others in their religion. There are other people who simply want to control believers for various reasons. The sad thing is that doing religious things for gain will void the grace that God extends to humans. Faith is the remedy to all of people's problems.

In the book of Romans, Paul tells the church how we should respond to the Spirit. Christianity is all about giving as we learn in this verse: *And so, dear brothers and sisters, I plead with you to give your bodies to God because of all he has done for you. Let them be* **a living and holy sacrifice**—*the kind he will find acceptable. This is truly the way to worship him. Romans 12:1* If we want to live with God in glory we must learn to suffer with Christ on earth. The straightforward answer is to give our body and soul to Jesus makes us the property of God. The new things we are asked to do must happen through a yielded body that is rightfully given to our Savior. In Galatians we read "It is no longer I who live, but Christ lives in me." We must allow the Spirit of God to totally direct our new life. A new power is in us and we will see great victories in our Christian life. Every victorious life will add to the unity of the Church.

Power is exercised by the Holy Spirit continually everywhere on earth. When Jesus was dead and in Hell great power was needed: *and he was shown to be the Son of God when he was raised from the dead* **by the power of the Holy Spirit.** *He is Jesus Christ our Lord. Romans 1:4* The power that was shown in the life of Jesus helped many people while in Israel but his location was limited. The power in a Christian life actually makes us into a supernatural person because we leave our old nature behind and live our life for God. Paul tells us how this happens: *For if you live by its dictates, you will die. But if through* **the power of the Spirit** *you put to death the deeds of your sinful nature, you will live. Romans 8:13* The world is catering to our sinful nature and we must put it to death which leaves time for us to live in the Spirit. By following the leading of the Spirit we can become righteous. We then are of value to God and to other people. Someday our devotion to God will be rewarded.

Christian thinking is obviously different than that of people enjoying this world. If we find ourselves agreeing with popular thinking we must run to the Lord in prayer and ask him to show us the truth of the subject. One aspect of our new thinking includes the connection that we feel with other saved people. We should humbly consider them as our honored family members. Remember we are never more important than any of the other brothers or sisters. Each of us is to help when others have needs. Some people fake concern for others and they are in danger of judgment. The Bible says: *They will act religious, but they **will reject the power** that could make them godly. ...2 Timothy 3:5* It is important that we be honest in every part of our Christian life. If you think loving people around us is tough remember that Jesus went even further. He said we must learn to love our enemies. The New Covenant can change any sinful person into a dedicated servant of God.

The church must return to the New Covenant way of serving God. It should be obvious to us that we will need a great deal of power beyond our own natural abilities. Providing power for the Covenant life of the church is a role of the Holy Spirit. The Bible says: *So we keep on praying for you, asking our God to enable you to live a life worthy of his call. **May he give you the power** to accomplish all the good things your faith prompts you to do. 2 Thessalonians 1:11* In the churches today we have many people feeling as if they can do nothing worthwhile for the kingdom of God. If this is true there is a simple answer. They have not tried to accomplish anything while living "in faith." The verse above reveals that the power will be given to us when godly things are being done by faith. If we will study the New Covenant and live in the Spirit we will find that the power is available for any of God's work.

Love is the command that Jesus gave to the church. This includes things like special consideration, a high regard, appreciation, admiration, respect, holding dear, generosity or charity among other things. It is quite common to show love through our actions because we cannot always create the suitable words. Of course Jesus showed his great love while on Earth. Today God shows his love to people through creation, scriptures, miracles or the Spirit living in Christians. Born again people all understand that we are part of the greatest act of love that ever happened. It began when the Spirit created Jesus in the womb of Mary. The book of John says: ***God showed how much he loved us** by sending his one and only Son into the world so that we might have eternal life through him. This is real love—not that we loved God, but that he loved us and sent his*

Son as a sacrifice to take away our sins. 1 John 4:9-10 Because of Jesus Christ the Holy Spirit now lives inside of every born again person.

God brings a special love into us through Jesus and the Spirit. This love is not available to a worldly person. In the Bible we learn that love is the highest attribute we can have. This is because God is Love. We would have nothing at all if Jesus had not clearly demonstrated what real love is. Love should be a priority in our life and the Holy Spirit makes it possible for every believer to be part of it. All the suffering in this world is has been caused by our enemy the Devil who hates everyone but some people still try to blame God for their problems. The fact that worldly people enjoy living with the enemy, who hates humans, is beyond my understanding. Paul said: *May you have the power to understand, as all God's people should, how wide, how long, how high, and how deep his love is. **May you experience the love of Christ**, though it is too great to understand fully... Ephesians 3:18-19* People who believe in God understand that he has a special love for those who serve in his household. There is no better master than Jesus our Savior.

Paul served God all his life but he never actually loved God until he met Jesus. He talks about how his old religion had no value in eternity: *If I gave everything I have to the poor and even sacrificed my body, I could boast about it; but if I didn't love others, **I would have gained nothing**. 1 Corinthians 13:3* Left alone the fallen human race can never find real love with God which is shown when we love others. We try to lead others to our Savior so they can find this love for themselves. Jesus came to earth to teach us that if we will love him, then we will find the true love of God. It is nice knowing that the love of God and Jesus will be ours when the Spirit resides in us. If believers today would realize who had come to live in them when they were saved it would be a completely different church that we attend. When a person accepts the love of our Savior it will sweep over them and their life will never be the same.

Unsaved people sometimes ask believers why there are so many Jesus signs at a ball game saying that God loves the whole world. This is because God has a general love for everything he has created. But this is not the individual love that the Savior has for each person who humbly serves him every day. When Jesus preached his first recorded sermon he taught us that God gave general love to the people of earth. ... *Pray for those who persecute you! In that way, you will be acting as true children of your Father in heaven. For **God gives his sunlight** to both the evil and the good, and **he sends rain** on the just and the unjust alike. Matthew 5:44-45* Jesus goes on to stress that his people will be different than all of the unredeemed. Further New Testament teaching says that because of the support God gives us in this world, we can successfully represent him as we reach out to the unsaved and tell them about the Savior. While serving Jesus we will mature in righteousness and support our brothers and sisters with love.

Chapter Six

Conscious of the Spirit

For many years the Church has failed to teach people about the Spirit that lives in us. Paul said that : ...*You are controlled by the Spirit if you have the Spirit of God living in you. (And remember that those who do not have the Spirit of Christ living in them do not belong to him at all.) Romans 8:*9 Every believer must develop their relationship with the Spirit of Jesus. Many humans are standing on the threshold of eternity without understanding that we must learn to be righteous. Even some believers are in danger of losing out on a life with God and they need to be warned. We have heard all our lives that the end was near but things seemed to continue the same as always. This has the overall effect of causing people to doubt the end will ever happen during their life. The fact is that anyone who is listening to the Spirit knows the actual time of the end has come. Awareness of the end even includes some worldly people who can see the clear signs. It is definitely time for every born again person to alert the people around them that they must not wait any longer to be serious about their salvation.

When an individual does seek Jesus for salvation and "the Lord accepts them" as his servant, the Spirit actually enters at that time. This is when the new believer talks about the great relief that came when the guilt of sin was lifted. We do not feel the Spirit as He enters us but the effects of the lifted guilt and things like love for people will begin to change our old attitudes. These changes will be noticeable to even the unsaved people around us. There are too many people being "saved" that have never felt a thing toward God or his forgiveness. The truth is that we should then begin to recognize the Spirit's work within us and learn to properly follow his leadership. The Spirit does work with both the saved and the unsaved.

For example the unsaved can normally feel some guilt in their soul. This is something that the Spirit has stirred up in them. Everything that the Spirit does will wait on the individual to yield their control to him. Hopefully the many end time warnings today will cause some people to ask how they can have the Holy Spirit's power be active in them.

Learning to yield to the will of God is something we must pray to receive. Our self-will is always wrong in the sight of God. A holy life is something that has been given completely to the Lord. Having a complete change of our life is a miracle and we must be ready to accept new attitudes and feelings. Depending on God is a wonderful life when entering fully in to it. The old way was to try and work everything out ourselves. But now we have faith and pray to God for his leadership in our daily walk. After our prayers are made there will be times when we must learn to patiently wait for the Spirit of God to do his work. A Christian never has the ability to tell God when he should do something. This would be a disaster because we have no idea how the changing of things will affect other lives spiritually. We don't even know how to fix things here on earth. God's answers are always perfect and waiting for him is actually an important part of faith.

A saved person must exercise their faith if they want to really know the Holy Spirit. Trusting the Holy Spirit is the only way to have consistent victory in your life. The Bible says that without faith we cannot please God. Recognizing and honoring the Spirit in our faith pleases the Father tremendously. For example, with our faith we quietly ask the Spirit how we should answer someone's questions. Before reading the Bible we invite the Spirit to give us the truth that we need. When our friend has a need we request the Spirit to work between them and Jesus. When we are involved with an accident our prayer will be that the Spirit inspires us with some way to help others or find an escape. If a friend of ours is heading toward hell we will ask the Spirit to repeatedly stir them to repent. In other words, we develop a relationship of dependence on him. Our life in Heaven will be based on the relationship we have with God on this earth.

Many believers don't know that the Spirit is responsible for our justification as well as our sanctification. That is important to a Christian!

Here's what the Scripture says: *And such were some of you: but ye are washed, but ye **are sanctified**, but ye **are justified** in the name of the Lord Jesus, **and by the Spirit of our God**. 1 Corinthians 6:11 (KJV)*. We must have our Savior but also the Holy Spirit because he facilitates every element of salvation. In this next verse Paul talks about the plan of God for us: *But we are bound to give thanks always to God for you, brethren beloved of the Lord, because God hath from the beginning chosen you to salvation **through sanctification of the Spirit** and belief of the truth: 2 Thessalonians 2:13 (KJV)* It will take a deliberate decision on our part to be led by the Spirit. Day after day we should decide by faith that the Spirit is our trusted guide.

The Spirit's leading will yield the victories and results that we want in our lives. Paul said: *For all who are **led by the Spirit** of God are children of God. Romans 8:14* Becoming a child of God forever is the greatest reward possible. The question some will ask is "what can I do to follow the Spirit?" The first thing that must happen is that we become like a dead person to all sin. Jesus made this possible on the cross. The Bible says: *We know that our old sinful selves were crucified with Christ so that **sin might lose its power** in our lives. We are no longer slaves to sin. For when we died with Christ we were set free from the power of sin. Romans 6:6-7* When a person is born again, God's power can take away the power of sin. We are no longer a slave to sin because a dead person cannot serve anyone. This allows righteousness to rule over our new life with the help of the Spirit.

Now that our internal compulsion for sin can be fought off but we must still watch out for the many attractions of this world. A born again person will consider themselves dead to the things that can distract us from serving the Lord. This is a matter of our dedication to God. Our witness is shown when we refuse to join the world's continual party. Paul said: *You have died with Christ, and he has set you free from **the spiritual powers of this world**. Colossians 2:20a* If we really want to be free from the power of our old nature and from the powers of this world it is now possible. This new freedom from the power of evil gives us the opportunity to tell everyone that we are serving Jesus. Scripture says: *For* *we died and were buried with Christ by baptism. And just as Christ was raised from the dead by the glorious power of the Father, now **we also may live** new lives. Romans 6:4* The new life that we have received can produce godly fruit because we have completely given ourselves to following the Spirit of God.

For 2000 years this subject of accepting our freedom in the Spirit is probably the biggest issue holding the entire church back from the victories God wants for them. Christians become content when they follow a routine in their life. We are made free so that our life will follow the Spirit into the adventures that God wants for us. The first church had the problem of retraining the converted Jews who had been trained to work hard at keeping "The Law." Paul had the difficult work of showing them that since Jesus had completed the work of the law they were now free to live in the Spirit. The American Christian was not trained in the Law of Moses but denominations will naturally gravitate toward various laws and routines of their own. Somehow all believers must learn that our righteous freedoms are found only in the guidance of God's Spirit. The Scriptures say: *For the Lord is the Spirit, and wherever the Spirit of the Lord is, **there is freedom.** 2 Corinthians 3:17* How wonderful it is that the Spirit brings the freedom to live righteously. Believers are in great need of accepting the freedom of Jesus as their way to serve God.

Another great hindrance to our freedom in Jesus is the worldliness that Christians have allowed into their lives. These people have misunderstood God's "freedom" and believe they are free to do anything allowed by their own seared conscience. When we ask Jesus to give us a new life it comes with a surrender of our conscience to the Holy Spirit. Christians have freedom from the evils of sin. They have freedom from the pain of worldly activities that have gone wrong. We are free from the fears of death that plague many people. Our freedom gives us a peaceful life that serves and pleases God. The Spirit uses our freedom to guide us in righteous ways. While teaching about our new life, Paul said: *Instead, let the Spirit renew your thoughts and attitudes. Put on your new nature, created to be like God—**truly righteous and holy**. Ephesians 4:23-24* Some people follow their own religious rules so they can leave room for the activities of their own choice. There is no way possible to follow the Spirit and please God while allowing any kind of sin in our life. We must find our freedom in the righteousness of Jesus.

Jesus through the Spirit is giving us a complete new life. It is our duty to claim it and never give up for any reason. This means we must continually renounce our own will and accept everything that the Lord wants for us. In other words we allow the Spirit to rule. This will give us time for everything God wants us to do. One of the things that people around us will enjoy is the truthfulness of all our behavior. The glory of God is being represented by the way we live. Christians will be honest even when they know that worldly people are planning to take advantage them. The Spirit already knows their evil plans and is far ahead of them. The Bible says: *So be happy when you are insulted for being a Christian, for then **the glorious Spirit of God rests upon you**. 1 Peter 4:14 God* will always win over the world even when we can't understand what he is doing. Many people say that God has given them wisdom and this makes their reasoning worth following. This is helpful but it's a mistake to use reason in place of God's will. Remember when all the wisdom was telling Paul not to go into Jerusalem. He had to inform everyone that the Spirit had instructed him to go anyway. (see Acts 21:10-14)

Unfortunately some people feel that they can live with some sin in their life because they were "forever" saved at age seven or twelve. These believers feel that the Almighty is obligated to save them because of the guarantee some preacher gave them in the past. God is not required to place backsliders in Heaven. Salvation is sacred and will be honored. Our salvation is completed by our lifelong faith and obedience. Our salvation only becomes a physical reality on the day we die. Peter said it this way: *And through **your faith**, God is protecting you by his power **until you receive this salvation**, which is ready to be revealed on the last day for all to see. 1 Peter 1:5* Today's church needs to wake up and live a new life of righteousness the way God has instructed us to do. There are people trying to teach this truth but the flood of selfish behavior and easy membership in our churches has overwhelmed the call for righteousness. Being a Christian is the greatest calling on earth but it is a calling by God. Let us be thrilled that the Spirit brings righteousness into our life.

Beginning our life of faith we will find that the Spirit leads us daily. The Spirit encourages our faith so we will seek a godly life. We must completely trust the promises of God. A human must accept the fact that God created them and that he really does love them. As children we had faith in our mom and dad. We did not understand everything but it was real to our little life. Of course the promises our parents will eventually let us down in some way. However when we find our reality in Jesus we can be certain that he will never betray us. People can only join God's family by having faith in Jesus even when they don't understand how it works. Some individuals can accept the love of the Savior very easily. But other folks have a great struggle with their "self." When salvation happens many people are surprised that their desires in life have suddenly changed. Now they want to live the new life that God has planned for them. The salvation message is about our need to accept the Lord as the leader of our life.

Choices are the dilemma of every natural life and can be frustrating to people who don't have faith in Jesus. Worldly folks want to choose a life of fun and parties, and then some of them want to be forgiven. So on Sunday they go to church hoping to be forgiven for their unrighteous life during the week. But a holy, godly life is absolutely necessary if we want to live in Heaven with God. This is a full time job. Actually, once a person is completely involved in serving Jesus they no longer desire the party life. Many church people like to say, "I believe, therefore I will live with God." But these same people refuse to say "I believe, so I will die to everything in this world." Saving faith includes both of these statements. The Scripture says it this way: *"Now if we died with Christ, we believe that we shall also live with Him." Romans 6:8* These two statements are two sides of the same coin. The dying must become true before the new life can exist. Many people have lost out on salvation simply because they will not give up their worldly ways for Jesus. We must choose one life or the other.

To be successful in the Christian life a person must wholeheartedly desire Jesus. When people did receive the knowledge of good and evil they did not receive the power to make every decision a good one. This leaves us with the only choice that can save us from ourselves. We must yield all our determinations to the spirit of Jesus who will always make godly choices for us. We have been taught for years that one decision is all we need for salvation. However the churches have accepted too many people that have misunderstood their "one" experience. The one decision of salvation is to yield all our choices to Jesus. Paul says that *YOU are slaves to sin, which leads to death, OR* (slaves) *to obedience, which leads to righteousness. Romans 6:16* It is the same question every individual must answer, "Who will control my thinking as I walk through life?" The Spirit is the power we need for a faith that ends with victory. It's difficult to explain but real Christians love to comply with the righteous ways of Jesus.

The love of God sent Jesus down to deal with our sin problem. But the decisions or choices we make in a natural life come from our own will. Out of all God's creations we are the only ones that have the free choice to live any way we want. Our decision must not come from cold logic. The salvation decision will happen because we desire God. When a person finally becomes saved it means they have yielded their choices in life to the Spirit of Jesus. This works well because the Spirit of Christ is in us and he directs the good decisions of faith that God must have for us to live in eternity with him. A Christian basically has given their responsibility of living a good life over to the Spirit of God. Of course we communicate with God and follow the instructions that he gives us. When a person leaves their decisions in His hands they can have a very faithful and righteous life. The same faith that the Spirit of Christ valued when he saved us is now used to follow his leading. This is why Christians can say they are walking in faith with Jesus.

Trusting the leading of the Spirit is the only secret to having a successful Christian life. The Bible says that in a life of faith: *All things work together for good to those who love God. Romans 8:28* This verse does not apply to the general public that claims to love God. It speaks to those who are walking in the light by yielding their life to the Spirit. People that give their life to the Savior have placed all their eggs in one basket we might say. No wonder regular people ask Christians why they can't join in with the things they are enjoying. It takes our honest faith to reject the pleasures of this world. When we make our own choices it is maintaining our old life of sin. There is no way to enjoy sin and remain in Christ. If we don't yield our decisions to the Spirit and we continue to make our own choices judgment day will be shocking. The remedy is to immediately confess every sin, repent and ask Jesus to forgive us. (See 1 John 1:9) Our old life has nothing important that is in common our new life of faith.

When we are tested or asked for a personal sacrifice it should be viewed as an opportunity to prove our commitment to the Lord. The five senses of our flesh will at times cause a weakening of our invisible faith. Never give these doubts enough consideration to erode our faith in Christ. God's possibilities for a righteous life will come through the channel of faith. The Bible tells us that all Spiritual fruit expresses the nature of Jesus. It should be obvious that the underlying reality of a believers hope will always be based on faith. Our Lord does not want us to have a backup plan. Give everything in our life over to Him, no matter how much it hurts to do it. This is the life of faith that we need. There will always be temptations but we can overcome them by asking the Spirit to show us the way to go. The sooner we get started trusting Jesus with our entire life the more we will enjoy the hope of our eternity and be living in the peace of our Creator. The Spirit will lead us to enter into "the rest of God."

The servants of Jesus must get rid of all doubt because it eats away at our faith. The Spirit of faith will develop the dedicated life that God wants for us. Christianity is not a life that is known to be full of caution or shyness. When a person goes all-in they are doing a bold thing. They have challenged the world who is continually trying to control us. It says you know that you hold the winning hand and you are depending on it. To trust in Jesus completely gives control to the Spirit and we find a wonderful freedom there. We need a Savior from ourselves. It's up to us to decide if we will continue in our selfish life or dedicate it to Jesus. Faith is an inner attitude of absolute reliance on the righteous God and continuing a relationship with Jesus is what develops our eternal place in the family of God. Each Christian has a position of value in God's eternal society. The more we exercise our faith, the closer we will be to the eternal life that fills our hope. Getting to know the Spirit is vitally important.

Chapter Seven

God's Vital Wisdom

Unbelievers have declared God dead. They have no idea how "alive" God is! Born again believers are very aware of the vitality of Jesus and the Spirit today. God has always guided the affairs of our history. Looking back to the Old Testament we read about the exploits of men who had the Spirit take over their body to perform the things that God required. Some of these men loved God but a few of them were not men of God at all. A good example is Moses and Pharaoh who represent these two different types of people. Moses was led by the Spirit but Pharaoh's rebellious spirit was used against him by the Spirit causing God's will to be done. People don't seem to realize that the Spirit, in those days, had the same unlimited power as he does today. Back then the Spirit usually brought a temporary condition to men that equipped them do his will. In the old days God seemed to be distant from people. It is completely different today because the Spirit is living in a believer and will stay with us forever. God joins his life with us which must be one of the biggest miracles ever preformed. When the Spirit comes into us we actually become more spiritually alive than anyone ever was in the Old Testament.

A fantastic part of this new living covenant is the fact that God ordained Paul to include Gentiles in the complete New Covenant way of the Spirit. (See Acts 9:17) The Jews were shocked when the Gentiles began to live and act out the gifts in the Spirit. They thought that God's Spirit was only for them. Gentiles and Jews could both live in the Spirit because his living Son now resides in all born again believers. The Old Testament people knew that the Spirit could overcome some person for a given time to accomplish a specific job. It could be any one that the Lord chose for the work he wanted done. Sometimes they did not even want the

Lord to use them like many believers today. The point is that the intimacy of the Spirit living in us today is far different than the limited experience that the Jews had in the past. The Jews were asked to live a righteous life with very little help from the Spirit. They memorized the Laws and tried their best to keep them day after day. It is our privilege to have all this personal help we have been studying. The Holy Spirit did come in a wonderful new way at Pentecost.

God "pours out his living Spirit" and the people he breathes on will begin to live a new life. We cannot see the Spirit but every individual is born again when the Spirit enters in to them. The advent of Jesus was the beginning of the legal procedure that God used to redeem and make people righteous again. The Spirit of God hovered over the Virgin Mary and the creation of our Savior was begun. Again the Spirit hovered over Jesus when he was baptized into his ministry. Then the Spirit came for Jesus when he ascended into Heaven. We know that the Spirit of God has always been working on this Earth. However the Day of Pentecost was special. It marked the day when the Spirit officially began to use the power and authority of the blood that Jesus had shed on the cross. Today the Spirit lives in redeemed people and enables our approved righteous life while giving us the power to bring redemption and healing to other people. This is unfolding the mysterious plan of God.

Long ago the Spirit came to the Jews in a way that was very exciting. It was the day they welcomed God's Spirit into the beautiful new Temple of Solomon. The Old Testament tells us: *Then the priests left the Holy Place. ...And the Levites who were musicians ... were dressed in fine linen robes and stood at the east side of the altar playing cymbals, lyres, and harps.* ***They were joined by 120 priests who were playing trumpets.*** *The trumpeters and singers performed together in unison to praise and give thanks to the LORD. ... At that moment a thick cloud filled the Temple of the LORD. The priests could not continue their service because of the cloud, for the glorious presence of the LORD filled the Temple of God. 2 Chronicles 5:11-14* These 120 priests were announcing the arrival of the Spirit who would live in the Temple. It is interesting that at Pentecost the glory of the Lord filled the upper room with flames of fire and 120 people began to announce that the power and glory of God had come to live in us. What God did for us is official and today we can have the power to live like Jesus.

These two special days of the Spirit were years apart and in very different ages but they were both important to God's great redemption plan. It is almost as if God's Spirit in the Old Covenant came with a thick smoke from a fire that was having a hard time burning. This smoke drove the ceremony out of the Temple. But the new covenant beginning at Pentecost had the flames of a mature fire that is burning cleanly. The people did not leave because the fire was cleanly burning in them. The power of our New Covenant made obsolete the old ceremonies on the day of Pentecost. This is why it is so important for Christians to live in the power of the New Covenant. The Old Covenant did not save: *For it is not possible for the blood of bulls and goats to take away sins. Hebrews 10:4* The old Law is certainly righteous but God wanted us all to see that no human could possibly keep all the demands. This was very hard on some of the Jews who had really tried. But God uses these old saints to teach us many lessons about our life. Thankfully today the Spirit has power for every need a Christian might have.

The Spirit directs not only an individual Christian but every genuine Church of faith in the world. Anywhere in the world Christians can follow the Lord as part of the one body of Christ. We are all tied into the same family because we follow the leading of the same Spirit. It is clear that Jesus had returned to Heaven before the Spirit began his important new job. He had no body until he entered humans and now he possesses the collective body of God's new family in Jesus. The righteous things that God wanted done during the next 2000 years would be done through the born again people who followed the directions of the Spirit. We must try to always work in the power of the Spirit: *I will send you the Advocate—the Spirit of truth. He will come to you from the Father and will testify all about me. And **you must also testify** about me ... John 15:26-27a* How much we yield to the Spirit will determine the amount of God's work in our life.

Peter began church ministry on the day of Pentecost. Our Bible tells us what he said that day: *Peter replied, "Each of you must repent of your sins, turn to God, and be baptized in the name of Jesus Christ to show that you have received forgiveness for your sins. **Then you will receive** the gift of the Holy Spirit. Acts 2:38* As soon as Jesus forgives our sins the Spirit will begin to live in side of us. If we will accept this power our service to God can benefit many people. Every person that is truly saved will want to be of service to God. That day Peter did not need to prepare his sermon, he just stood up and spoke what the Spirit wanted him to say. There were many different languages in the crowd that day but the Spirit spoke to every person so they could understand. We read: *Those who believed what Peter said were baptized **and added** to the church that day—about 3,000 in all. Acts 2:4* History continued by showing us how the Spirit used people to build the church for the last 2000 years.

Of course the Holy Spirit is invisible and this makes it impossible to really explain him to people who don't have him living in them. All the years since Jesus left earth the Spirit has been working through special people to be continually building the family of God. We can read about the struggles it took to get the local churches going in the book about the Acts of the Spirit and the early Christian pioneers. One day Peter told the authorities: *We are witnesses of these things and so is the Holy Spirit, who is given by God to **those who obey him**." Acts 5:32* It is very sad for a church to operate without acknowledging the leadership of the Spirit. Christians must teach each following generation that a new spiritual life is only available to people who allow the Spirit to lead there life. This includes how they will produce fruit for the kingdom of God. Remember, the seed will fall on four kinds of soil but only the fourth soil produces a crop. People are the soil and without some good soil there cannot be a harvest.

The Spirit can do many things at once. For example while he is teaching, leading, and comforting individual Christians he is also able to coordinate the church work. With a group of Spirit filled people the Spirit can build a real power filled house of salvation. With this group of dedicated servants the Spirit will accomplish things as if Jesus himself were here on earth. This was the secret of the first century church and many things were done for God. The Spirit is doing things all around the world today through the servants of God. The Bible says: *All of you together are Christ's body, and **each of you is a part** of it. 1 Corinthians 12:27* In America we have millions of "believers" who live only to themselves and will not even meet with others in a local gathering. They claim that they are better Christians than the ones who gather. The real question they should answer is why the Spirit would "lead" them to live apart from other believers? Are their hearts being hardened to God's will for them?

Some Christians will say "We can do everything better at home." A few of them even plan their marriages and funerals without the local church. But let's look at a few scriptures about the church. In these last days we must stay with others so that we can encourage each other to keep our lives full of righteousness. Paul gave this warning: *You must **warn each other** every day, while it is still "today," so that none of you will be deceived by sin and hardened against God. For if we are faithful to the end, trusting God just as firmly as when we first believed, **we will share in all** that belongs to Christ. Remember what it says: "Today when you hear his voice, don't harden your hearts as Israel did when they rebelled." Hebrews 3:13-15* This passage is full of concern for others which is necessary for every group of Christians. Someday we will share in the inheritance of Jesus and it will be good to see many others rejoicing with us.

As we wait for Jesus we can all get tired at times. The truth is that we all need to occasionally be told to get up and keep going. If we will stir up the gifts that are in us then along with others we can make it. Remember that no one goes to Heaven individually: *For the Lord himself will come down from heaven with a commanding shout, with the voice of the archangel, and with the trumpet call of God. First, the Christians who have died will rise from their graves. **Then, together with them,** we who are still alive and remain on the earth will be caught up in the clouds to meet the Lord in the air. Then we will be with the Lord forever. So encourage each other with these words. 1 Thessalonians 4:16-18* There are many ways that belonging to a church is valuable for us. The church sends our money to support missionaries. Even greeting each other with the love of the Lord encourages people who may be having a hard time. We should do our best to make Jesus "real" in our own life and for others.

When Paul was saying goodbye to one of his churches he warned them to look after their brothers and sisters. We are responsible for other people who love God: *"So guard yourselves **and God's people**. Feed and shepherd God's flock—his church, purchased with his own blood—over which the Holy Spirit has appointed you as elders. Acts 20:28* The reason most people stay at home and neglect other Christians is laziness. It's true that this is addressed to our leaders but saying we are responsible to help others and it will please God. All believers should ask the Spirit to show them a person they can help in our church. This is not a decision that we should make with our mind alone. As with all our work it is important that we pray for God to show us the person and how to help. When we learn to listen for the directions of God our spiritual life will grow. The purpose of a Christian life is to grow and mature into a loving family member in God's Kingdom.

The New Testament is written with the assumption that we will be together with others as we grow in the Lord. It usually tells us things that we do along with others. For example the Spirit helps us to sing many wonderful things to God. We do this with other people indicated by the plural form of "hearts." *Let the message about Christ, in all its richness, fill your lives. Teach and counsel **each other** with all the wisdom he gives. Sing psalms and hymns and spiritual songs to God with thankful **hearts**. Colossians 3:16* Worshiping together is very much an activity that we enjoy with other people. The wisdom of God has asked us to help the weak members and it takes the Spirit's help. It's true that it can be difficult without the Spirit of love. Human relationships do become frayed very quickly but a group of spirit-filled people will love each other forever. If some of them die we will miss them until we get back together in Heaven. What a great reunion that will be!

When the Spirit is in a church great things can happen among the members. James was the elder of a great church and he said this: *Are any of you suffering hardships? You should pray. Are any of you happy? You should sing praises. Are any of you sick? You should call for **the elders of the church to come and pray over you,** anointing you with oil in the name of the Lord. Such a prayer offered in faith will heal the sick, and the Lord will make you well. And if you have committed any sins, you will be forgiven. James 5:13-15* This verse makes no sense if we try to apply it to people who think they don't need anybody else around them. Peter tells us that we should seek others because of a bond that was created when Jesus suffered and died to save us. The bond is our thankfulness for being saved from living in Hell. This should cause us to love others and even be willing to die for them. The Spirit can even do this in us if we seek a loving fellowship. Are we grateful enough to Jesus for the way he suffered and died for us?

Paul explains that we should try to help believers who have fallen into sin again. To share your strength with a weaker believer is the right thing to do. This is a lot different than refusing to worship with people who are not "on your level." Scripture says: *Share each other's burdens, and in this way obey the law of Christ. If you think you are too important to help someone, you are only fooling yourself. **You are not that important**. Galatians 6:2,3* This passage continues by saying that we will be held responsible for the way we love others. The church gives an opportunity for all the gifts to operate as we help others. Our local church is a part of the collective church located all around the world. Thankfully the Spirit gives gifts, such as preaching, that are good anywhere the Lord leads. A preacher can use his gift everywhere in the world but we are told that love is above all of the other gifts from the Spirit.

Christians are called into the church at salvation and it is a lifelong challenge. The Bible says: *This will continue until we all come to such unity in our faith and knowledge of God's Son **that we will be mature in the Lord**, measuring up to the full and complete standard of Christ. Ephesians 4:13* The Spirit certainly has his work cut-out with some of us. Because we are told that love is higher than all of the gifts from the Spirit it certainly must be taken seriously. Along with our local church we should desire the best worship to build us up for our witness to the world. The Bible says: *After this prayer, the meeting place shook, and they were all filled with the Holy Spirit.* **Then they preached the word of God with boldness.** *Acts 4:31* Yielding ourselves to the Spirit will involve singing, praying, studying along with others. The fact is that we must worship with others if we want to love God in the purest form.

Of course the Lord wants to hear from each of us individually. The Spirit is God and this means that everything a fully dedicated believer does is worshiping the Lord. When we serve God with all our life it is because God is fully deserving of it and everything we do in the Spirit is worship. There is not one good thing in which God does not deserve our wonder and honor. He actually is everything good that exist. The truth is that the church needs leadership more than they do an order of worship. The church and the individual must honor God first with their worship. Jesus tells us: *But the time is coming—indeed it's here now—when true worshipers will* **worship the Father in spirit** *and in truth. The Father is looking for those who will worship him that way. John 4:23* Real worship to God only comes from the heart of people and not from some religious order. We must see the importance of our whole heartedness for God.

Christians know that Jesus died so that humans could have a return to personal fellowship with the Father. The Savior provided the blood 2000 years ago but we must pursue God and reach a place of fellowship with him. The Bible says: *Now all of us can* **come to the Father through the same Holy Spirit** *because of what Christ has done for us. Ephesians 2:18* The Spirit of fellowship did not provide the blood but he does utilize everything the Savior paid for. The Spirit is invisible and he quietly helps us with every spiritual aspect of our life. Our part is to become a vessel that will yield both their thinking and their limbs to the leading of the Holy Spirit. Paul is clear that we are saved by death and by life: *For since our friendship with God was* **restored** *by the death of his Son while we were still his enemies, we will certainly be* **saved** *through the life of his Son. Romans 5:10* (both are brought to us by the spirit as seen above) The Spirit and Jesus are enabling us to become a Christian who can please

God by doing his work.

Living with the Spirit active in our life is a real joy. Day or night we can interact with Jesus who has done so much for us that it is not possible to keep track. And when we add this to what he is doing in his church it is certainly more than we can grasp. All of this leads in a continual chorus of thanksgiving to our God. Gentiles can now enjoy the Lord: *For we who **worship by the Spirit** of God are the ones who are truly circumcised. We rely on what Christ Jesus has done for us. ... Philippians 3:3* When the church prays together, our joy and thanksgiving will increase. Church prayer benefits the preaching and teaching that are done in the Spirit. Paul said: *Always be joyful. Never stop praying. **Be thankful in all circumstances**, for this is God's will for you who belong to Christ Jesus. Do not stifle the Holy Spirit. 1 Thessalonians 5:16-19* Anything we do without the Spirit will grieve him. Whatever order of service we have it must not interfere with the Spirit and our true worship of God.

Chapter Eight

Wisdom for Our New Life

Human wisdom is selfish and usually hard on the people receiving advice. Many times wisdom will lead individuals to be proud and indifferent toward God. Some people with human wisdom become unbearable because of their arrogance. It is great to know that the wisdom of the Spirit is completely different. The Bible tells us: *But **the wisdom from above** is first of all pure. It is also peace loving, gentle at all times, and willing to yield to others. It is full of mercy and good deeds. It shows no favoritism and is always sincere. James 3:17* This new wisdom makes Christians into unusual people that we love to be around. One definition of wisdom is to choose the best course of action. A believer can easily understand that Jesus is the best course of action for any situation. The rational thoughts of humans are so far beneath what God has for us that there is really no comparison. Reading the first three chapters of Corinthians will clearly spell out what God thinks about the wisdom of people.

The collective wisdom of humans is not any more spiritual than the one person. In the world today we gather in groups of people thinking that the sum of our reasoning is certainly better than listening to God. Human wisdom of many people will always fail and for proof of this just look at our country today. It is important that Churches rely on the wisdom of the Spirit. No matter how large or small the decision God's wisdom is always correct. The Scripture says: *There the child grew up healthy and strong. **He was filled with wisdom**, and God's favor was on him. Luke 2:40* We know that the Spirit was part of the conception and wisdom came to earth with Jesus. The original church in Jerusalem made this decision to care for their members: *And so, brothers, select seven men* who are well respected and are **full of the Spirit and wisdom**. *We will give them this responsibility. Acts 6:3* They knew what kind of men had real wisdom and were able to love rather than judge. The early church had the wisdom of the Spirit.

Today we are actually in the beginning of the seven year tribulation but we will be saved out of every situation by godly wisdom. Bad things might happen to us but we stay in Jesus and never give in to fear. The Word tells us that Christians will be taken before worldly judges which can be frightening. Jesus left instructions for us: *So don't worry in advance about how to answer the charges against you, for **I will give you the right words** and **such wisdom** that none of your opponents will be able to reply or refute you! Luke 21:14-15* The Spirit is necessary if we are to have a powerful witness for Christ. Everything about living a life of faith requires the wisdom of God. The Bible says: *But to those called by God to salvation, both Jews and Gentiles, **Christ is** the power of God and **the wisdom of God.** 1 Corinthians 1:24* Any decision that needs to be made must have prayers asking for wisdom. Even in the Old Testament righteous decisions were made for the Lord's people by God.

For example, Christians should listen to the Spirit during the selection of their preacher. One of the problems today is that many of them are preaching for the money and they are difficult to identify. We must be led to a man that relies on the Spirit of truth and wisdom for their guidance. To be clear these men rely on their reasoning or what the Bible calls "man's wisdom." This will lead people astray even if they did not intend it originally. Only the Spirit can tell us the truth about an unknown preacher. The Bible says: *For when we brought you the Good News, it was not only with words but also with power, **for the Holy Spirit** gave you full assurance that what we said was true. ... 1 Thessalonians 1:5* We must build our spiritual confidence from the wisdom of the Spirit and not from any preacher or leader. Paul taught that the enticing words of these preachers were profane in the House of God. (see- 1 Corinthians 1:18-31) Carefully ask the Lord to give you the right man who follows the Holy Spirit and knows that Christ is the wisdom of God.

The wise preacher will pray and study the whole truth of the Gospel. He should not continually preach the parts that he is comfortable with. The salvation plan of God is absolutely wonderful and because of the Spirit we know more about it today than ever before. Peter said: *This salvation was something even the prophets wanted to know more about when they prophesied about this gracious salvation prepared for you. They wondered what time or situation the Spirit of Christ within them was talking about when he told them in advance about Christ's suffering and his great glory afterward. They were told that their messages were not for themselves, but for you. And now this Good News has been announced to you by those who **preached in the power of the Holy Spirit** sent from heaven. It is all so wonderful that even the angels are eagerly watching these things happen. 1 Peter 1:10-12* How much preaching is about our suffering for Jesus? It is now possible for us to live a wise and joyful life during any conditions and the angels will celebrate along with us.

Today we have many Christians who ignore the Spirit because they are afraid to show their emotions. This is pride and it stands in the way of God's wisdom. Jesus is the wisdom of God and getting emotional is one way to honor God. Christians are never ashamed of the Lord and emotions show that we love him. When people adore earthly activities they don't mind showing their emotions. It is wise for a Christian to accept that the Spirit of Jesus enjoys the different ways that people worship him. Someday in Heaven all believers will behave with great emotion: *Then I heard again what sounded like **the shout of a vast crowd** or the roar of mighty ocean waves or the crash of loud thunder:* (saying) *"Praise the LORD! For the Lord our God, the Almighty, reigns. Revelation 19:6* Spirit led emotion is pure and wholesome. It is true that when we are in a crowd our behavior should benefit the people around us. Part of our prayer and worship in a crowd is dedicated to the people around us. We are not alone.

When the Spirit moves with humans many times unusual things happen. We must not be concerned and question the Lord. No matter what our reasoning is it is our work to support the Spirit's work with other people. Here is what we are told to do: *Pray **in the Spirit at all times** and*

on every occasion. Stay alert and be persistent in your prayers for all
believers everywhere. Ephesians 6:18* Christians should be consistently
positive about the Lord. The church spends too much time criticizing
when they should be proclaiming their faith in Christ. The work of God is
huge and each of us can choose to do as much work for the Lord as we
want. The Bible says: *But you, dear friends, must build each other up in
your most holy faith,* **pray in the power** *of the Holy Spirit,* **and await the
mercy** *of our Lord Jesus Christ, who will bring you eternal life. In this
way, you will keep yourselves safe in God's love. Jude 1:20-21* The more
we dedicate our mind and body to God the greater spiritual life we will
have.

The wisdom of God is so great that no human could possibly hold
it. The goodness of God allows the Spirit to reveal what we need at just
the right time. The perfect virtues of the Lord mean that every bit of
wisdom given to us will be perfect. This is why we are required to listen
carefully to the directions of the Spirit. Jesus is the wisdom that our world
needs so badly. Today's Church is being separated into those that are
willing to suffer for Jesus and those who selfishly worship their own
thinking. The comfortable religions of today are not of God. Scripture
says: *Dear friends, don't be surprised at the fiery trials you are going
through, as if something strange were happening to you. Instead, be very
glad—for these trials make you partners with Christ in his suffering, so
that you will have the wonderful joy of seeing his glory when it is revealed
to all the world. So be happy when you are insulted for being a Christian,
for then* **the glorious Spirit of God rests upon you.** *1 Peter 4:12-14* Real
wisdom is obeying the Word of God and honoring Jesus our Savior.

The Spirit of wisdom and worship is the work most suited to the
Holy Spirit. Because he is God with perfect understanding of everything
he knows exactly how to lead people in worship. Paul tells us how we
have a place in God's kingdom: *Don't you realize that all of you together
are the temple of God and that the Spirit of God lives in you? God will
destroy anyone who destroys this temple. For God's temple is holy, and
you are that temple. 1 Corinthians 3:16-17* Think of the Spirit as the
mortar between all the bricks used in God's Temple. This places him in a

position to lead our collective worship perfectly. The body of Jesus will naturally praise God with a unified voice. Wonderful times will happen because of the Spirit's influence. The Bible says: *When they reached the place where the road started down the Mount of Olives, all of his* **followers began to shout and sing** *as they walked along, praising God for all the wonderful miracles they had seen. Luke 19:37* God loves these times with his people.

Christians find that wisdom leads directly into ministry. Our whole life is worshiping God first and then ministering to other people as the Spirit directs us. We know that Jesus is our example so we look at his ministry. He did not withhold any of it from our life because we have the same Spirit. In fact he said that we might even do greater things if God willed it. After the Savior was baptized with the Spirit of God we read: *Then Jesus returned to Galilee,* **filled with the Holy Spirit's power.** *Reports about him spread quickly through the whole region. Luke 4:14* and *Luke 4:18-19* **"The Spirit of the LORD is upon me,** *for he has anointed me to bring Good News to the poor. He has sent me to proclaim that captives will be released, that the blind will see, that the oppressed will be set free, and that the time of the LORD's favor has come."* It is obvious here that the power of God's wisdom led directly into the ministry of Jesus.

The church today really needs to find their first love and display it to others in these last days. Christians have the wisdom of eternity. The great prophet John the Baptist was asked many questions about what he was declaring to be the new life for believers. *John answered their questions by saying, "I baptize you with water; but someone is coming soon who is greater than I am—so much greater that I'm not even worthy to be his slave and untie the straps of his sandals.* **He will baptize you with the Holy Spirit and with fire.** *Luke 3:16* He goes on to say that God will burn up the wasted chaff in a fire that will never go out and this will keep his wheat pure. Are believers today being serious about their dedication to God? The living water is not only poured into us but it must flow on through us into the world around us. The living water that flow through a person is most satisfying. It brings joy into a dedicated life at every situation we might find ourselves in.

The world finds happiness in their time of reveling or temporary success. But that is very different than the gladness and contentment of a godly life with its hope of eternity. Paul spoke of his continual joy: *Our hearts ache, but we always have joy. **We are poor,** but we give spiritual riches to others. **We own nothing**, and yet we have everything. 2 Corinthians 6:10* The things that seemed so important when we were in the world will grow strangely dim. The Spirit can change our original attitude until we at times forget our condition before salvation. We have been relieved of all worry and it allows us to relax and enjoy life. Scripture says: *Let everyone see that you are considerate in all you do. Remember, the Lord is coming soon. Don't worry about anything; instead, pray about everything. Tell God what you need, and thank him for all he has done. Philippians 4:5-6* This teaching is completely about our new God given wisdom.

King David loved to play his harp and sing joyfully to the Lord. He said this: *How the king rejoices in your strength, O LORD! **He shouts with joy** because you give him victory. For you have given him his heart's desire; you have withheld nothing he requested. Psalm 21:1-2* Christians are able to praise the Lord at any time and the Spirit enables us to have a great day. David continues by saying: *I will be glad and rejoice in your unfailing love, for you have seen my troubles, and you care about the anguish of my soul. Psalm 31:7* Cheering up the world around us is something every believer should be doing. The Scripture tells us why: *Let the godly sing for joy to the LORD; it is fitting for the pure to praise him. Psalm 33:1* There are many wonderful ways to experience the "joy of the Lord" and Christians should find their happiness and share it with the world around them.

When Jesus was teaching his disciples about the Spirit he had to limit what he said. Here is what we are told: *(When he said "living water," he was speaking of the Spirit, who would be given to everyone believing in him. But **the Spirit had not yet been given**, because Jesus had not yet entered into his glory.) John 7:39* This story has a happy ending however because the Spirit did come later. A year or two after Jesus was killed a new convert by the name of Paul was directed into the Arabian Desert (probably the mountain where God gave Moses the Law.) He personally met with Jesus himself and received the rest of the information that God wanted us to have about the Holy Spirit. Our God works in mysterious and wonderful ways. Look at the amazing end of our life: ... *we want to put on our new bodies so that these dying bodies will be swallowed up by life.* **God himself has prepared us for this,** *and as a* guarantee **he has given us his Holy Spirit.** *2 Corinthians 5:4b-5* Notice that God prepared us for the transition into this new body by giving us the Holy Spirit.

Here are some other examples of how the Spirit can lead Christians. God gave us a book about the Acts of the Holy Spirit. --- *A prophet named Agabus stood up in one of the meetings and* **predicted by the Spirit** *that a great famine was coming upon the entire Roman world. (This was fulfilled during the reign of Claudius.)* Acts 11:28 --- *One day as these men were worshiping the Lord and fasting,* **the Holy Spirit said,** *"Dedicate Barnabas and Saul for the special work to which I have called them."* Acts 13:2 --- *Then coming to the borders of Mysia, they headed north for the province of Bithynia,* **but again the Spirit of Jesus** *did not allow them to go there.* Acts 16:7. The Spirit tells us thousands of details for our life that are too specific to be in the Scriptures. This is where the "Scripture only" people are making a mistake. Getting to know the Spirit's voice is a very big part of the new covenant. This gives real wisdom and power to our ministry.

Isaiah 30:21 Your own ears will hear him. **Right behind you a voice will say,** *"This is the way you should go,"* *whether to the right or to the left.*

Chapter Nine

Magnificent Gifts

While Apollos was in Corinth, Paul traveled through the interior regions until he reached Ephesus, on the coast, where he found several believers. "Did you receive the Holy Spirit when you believed?" he asked them. "No," they replied, "we haven't even heard that there is a Holy Spirit." "Then what baptism did you experience?" he asked. And they replied, "The baptism of John." Paul said, "John's baptism called for repentance from sin. But John himself told the people to believe in the one who would come later, meaning Jesus." As soon as they heard this, they were baptized in the name of the Lord Jesus. **Then when Paul laid his hands on them, the Holy Spirit came on them,** *and they spoke in other tongues and prophesied. There were about twelve men in all.*

Acts 19:1-7

But now the people believed Philip's message of Good News concerning the Kingdom of God and the name of Jesus Christ. As a result, many men and women were baptized. Then Simon himself believed and was baptized. He began following Philip wherever he went, and he was amazed by the signs and great miracles Philip performed. When the apostles in Jerusalem heard that the people of Samaria had accepted God's message, they sent Peter and John there. As soon as they arrived, they prayed for these new believers to receive the Holy Spirit. The Holy Spirit had not yet come upon any of them, for they had only been baptized in the name of the Lord Jesus. **Then Peter and John laid their hands upon these believers, and they received the Holy Spirit.**

Acts 8:12-17

Regrettably the greatest witness of Jesus and the Holy Spirit has disappeared in most American churches. Men of the cloth have forbidden the signs of power available to Christians. God graciously gave Christians these manifestations of power to help unbelieving people actually see the reality of our God. The fact that people receive any benefit from them is secondary to the display of God's goodness which brings glory to his name. Most of these unbelieving churches will tell you that God did not continue manifestations after the first century. There is absolutely nothing in the Scriptures to support this man made reasoning. In third world countries the Spirit does all these same works today. There is no good work that God has ever given to Christians and then taken it away from them. Most likely the leaders of the church could not control what God was doing so they decided to ban it from churches. Today's American church discarded the miraculous gifts because they don't fit in to their order of services.

God gave miracles so that his power could be seen by the unbelievers and his church would honor him. But our enemy is always trying to make God disappear from our worship. Some people wanted Paul to stay away but he told them: *When I was with you, I certainly **gave you proof that I am an apostle**. For I patiently did many signs and wonders and miracles among you. 2 Corinthians 12:12* We are supposed to have proof that we are Christians. Sadly Paul told Timothy that in the last days our church would be powerless and our churches are making this come true today. Believers are aware that only certain people regularly display these wonderful power gifts but for us to refuse to let God's gifts into our church is a sin. Of course all the gifts are available to any Christian when they call out to God for his help. The church leaders today point out that they do not need chaos in their gatherings because it disturbs God. This certainly does not bother God but the Spirit did have Paul give some rules for church use of gifts. (See: 1 Corinthians 12)

There are gifts for everyday Christians that don't seem as powerful as some of the special ones. Everyone should develop these as part of our daily life. The Spirit will lead us in these every day gifts that are part of a believers new life. The Scripture says: *In his grace, **God has given us***

different gifts *for doing certain things well. So if God has given you the ability to prophesy, speak out with as much faith as God has given you. If your gift is serving others, serve them well. If you are a teacher, teach well. If your gift is to encourage others, be encouraging. If it is giving, give generously. If God has given you leadership ability, take the responsibility seriously. And if you have a gift for showing kindness to others, do it gladly. Romans 12:6-8* The truth is that there are no limits on the Spirit of God and every Christian should enjoy the freedom of believing everything is possible in their Godly life. It is fear and lack of faith that withholds the miracles that are intended for the church.

The gifts by nature will protect us from fear. Having spiritual power gives us confidence and the fears around us just fade away. The Scripture says: *This is why I remind you to fan into flames the spiritual gift God gave you when I laid my hands on you. For God has not given us a spirit of fear and timidity,* ***but of power****, love, and self-discipline. 2 Timothy 1:6-7* Paul said that Christians are given a Spirit of power. If this is true then why are church people quietly slipping in and out of the church meetings where the power is forbidden. When we are living like Jesus "all" fear will disappear from our life. The Bible says: *Such love has no fear, because perfect love expels all fear. If we are afraid, it is for fear of punishment, and this shows that we have not fully experienced his perfect love. We love each other because he loved us first. 1 John 4:18-19* Once again we see that love is at the bottom of our relationship with God. We should learn to love more every day.

It was a remarkable day for modern believers when Jesus walked down to the river for his baptism and began the most wonderful ministry ever accomplished in history. Everything Jesus ever did while on this earth was clearly done to benefit the human race. The Scripture tells us there was great power in his ministry: *And you know that God anointed Jesus of Nazareth with* ***the Holy Spirit and with power****. Then Jesus went around doing good and healing all who were oppressed by the devil, for God was with him. Acts 10:38* His simple water baptism confirmed that Jesus was the one who intended to give his life and death for our salvation while he lived in the Spirit. The descending of the Holy Spirit on Jesus did verify that the Spirit would be a part of his ministry. Everyone has a different amount of power but Jesus of course had the greatest faith and power of any human. We, as followers of Jesus Christ, do have the opportunity to ask the Spirit increase our own faith and power.

The power of God caused complete success in the ministry of Jesus because we can see the confidence of his prayers and read the results. After Pentecost the Spirit will do the same for all the believers who will trust in his power. It is amazing to experience the Holy Spirit's power in our own ministry. There are millions of Christians in the world today and the surveys show that about half of them are privileged to have had a special baptism of the Spirits power in their life. Ministry power leads us to show others the "living" Gospel. The power of the Spirit should be part of who we are in Jesus. The Bible says: *Jesus Christ is the same yesterday, today, and forever. Hebrews 13:8* If Jesus lives in a Christian then they should have the same kind of ministry. Jesus came to show us how to live the Christian life. The Savior lived every one of his days in the power of the Spirit. Anyone who denies the miracle power is saying that God is not truthful with us.

The Spirit of God has all the power needed for our ministry. The amazing thing is that puny little humans have the right to say no to the power of God in their life. Every human can say "no" to the power of salvation, and likewise saved people can say "no" to any spiritual power. It is always our decision on how much we want to love God. The more we love him the more we will have power to lead people to God. Paul tells us that even believers who have accepted the Spirit's gifts are still in control of their decisions. The Scripture says: *Remember that people who prophesy **are in control** of their spirit and can take turns. 1 Corinthians 14:32* Unfortunately there is a great deal of disagreement about the Spirit having the ability to add gifts beyond salvation. This argument has left the church partially made up of "second blessing Christians" while others are "Salvation only Christians." Most third-world believers need and they do receive the Spirit's gifts. However wealthy nations who have more comfort for themselves like money and insurance don't want to experience these unusual gifts. They are afraid to trust God.

Here are two Scriptures that help us see the reality of the Spirit: *Jesus replied, "I assure you, no one can enter the Kingdom of God without being born of water and the Spirit. Humans can reproduce only human life, but **the Holy Spirit gives birth to spiritual life**. John 3:5-6* Clearly the Holy Spirit somehow enters a person and gives them their new birth. We certainly know that Jesus already had salvation, but John tells us that the Holy Spirit came into him: *I didn't know he was the one, but when God sent me to baptize with water, he told me, 'The one on whom you see **the Spirit descend** and rest is the one who will **baptize with the Holy Spirit**.' John 1:33* Jesus certainly received "the second blessing" and we also need all the power available to minister for God. It seems logical that in addition to the power that saved us, it is certain that God gave us other gifts. The Gospels tell us about the power of the Spirit that was seen throughout the ministry of Jesus. Whatever you decide about the Spirit's power be sure you love other people in the Lord. Love will certainly cover many other things.

Every believer must develop their own relationship with the Spirit. Many believers are standing on the threshold of eternity without knowing the Holy Spirit. Some church people are even in danger of losing out on a life with God and they need to be warned. All our lives we have heard that the end was near but things continued on the same as always. This has the overall effect of causing people to believe the end will never happen during their life. The fact is that anyone who is listening to the Spirit knows the actual time of the end has come. Awareness of the end even includes some worldly people who can see the clear signs. It is definitely time for the last generation. Every born again person should alert the people around them that they must not wait any longer to be serious about their salvation. Only the Spirit can lead us successfully to Heaven.

Hopefully this end time warning might cause some people to ask how they can have the Holy Spirit active in them. He becomes active when we make a move in faith. Just like when we moved in faith on the day of our salvation. When an individual seeks Jesus for salvation and the Lord accepts them as his servant the Spirit actually enters at that time. This is when the new believer talks about the great relief that came when the guilt of sins was lifted from off them. We do not feel the Spirit as he enters us however the effects of the lifted guilt and things like love for people will begin to change our old feelings. These changes will be noticeable to even the unsaved people around us. Christians must begin to recognize the Spirit's work within us and learn to properly follow his leadership. The Spirit does a different work with the unsaved. For example they can normally feel some guilt in their soul. This is something that the Spirit has stirred up in them. Everything that the God does will wait on the individual to yield their control to the Spirit of Jesus Christ.

Learning to yield to the will of God is a secret we must learn. Our will is always wrong in the sight of God. A holy life is something that has been given completely to the Lord. Having a complete change of our life is a miracle and we must be ready to accept new attitudes and feelings. Depending on God is a wonderful life when entering fully in to it. The old way was to try and work everything out ourselves. But now we have faith in our prayers to God. After our prayers are made we must learn to faithfully wait for the Spirit of God to do his work. A Christian never has the ability to tell God when he should do something. This would be a disaster because we have no idea how the changing of things will affect other lives spiritually. We don't even know how to fix things here on earth. God's answers are always perfect and waiting for him is an important part of faith. Perseverance is waiting patiently on God.

A saved person actually must exercise their faith if they want to really know the Holy Spirit. Knowing the Holy Spirit is the only way to have consistent victory in our lives. The Bible says that without faith we cannot please God. Recognizing and honoring the Spirit in our faith pleases the Father tremendously. Paul said this to his friend: *This is why I remind you to fan into flames **the spiritual gift God gave you when I laid my hands on you.*** *2 Timothy 1:6* For example, with our faith we quietly ask the Spirit how we should deal with someone's request. A mature Christian will ask the Spirit to give us the help that we need. Everyone should ask the Spirit to bring Jesus into their situation. For example if we are involved with an accident, our prayer will be that the Spirit inspires us with some way to help another or to find a solution to save them. And when a friend of ours is heading toward hell we will ask the Spirit to repeatedly stir them to repent. In other words, we develop a relationship of dependence on the Spirit. Our life in heaven is going to be organized around our relationship with God on this earth.

We should know the power of God comes through our faith that the Spirit has given each of us at salvation. We are part of a union with the whole trinity. Christians are now a fourth part in the family of God. Do we believe we are part of his family or not? Jesus said to us: *"I tell you the truth, **anyone who believes in me will do the same works I have done,** and even greater works, because I am going to be with the Father. John 14:12* When living as a human Jesus said he had done miracles when the actual power was supplied by the Spirit. Everyone involved with the plan of God does different things but we are all a part of the whole. Paul did powerful actions that the Spirit had obviously supplied. Why don't we tell people of powerful things that we have done that are powered by the Spirit of God? Christians have been adopted into the powerful family of God and they should love being a part of this magnificent dynasty. Every Christian should show that they belong to this family while leading others to our great and powerful God. When we love the trinity we are representing them to the needy world. This is the will of God for every one of his children.

A big reason why we need the power of the Spirit is because we have a strong enemy by the name of Satan. His domain is in the space around earth which places him and his followers personally in between us and God. He wants to destroy everyone who serves God because he has declared that he deserves to rule in God's place. The Holy Spirit defends our life from this evil individual. One of Satan's favorite tricks is to tell us lies. The Bible warns us: *Stay alert! Watch out for your great enemy, the devil. He prowls around like a roaring lion, looking for someone to devour. 9 Stand firm against him, and **be strong in your faith.** ... 1 Peter 5:8-9* Our faith must be used to show others that we know our Lord is far more powerful. We remember the great power of the spirit that lived in Jesus as he helped people. *When they left, a demon-possessed man who couldn't speak was brought to Jesus. So **Jesus cast out the demon, and*** *then the man began to speak. The crowds were amazed. ... Matthew 9:32-33* Satan had ruined this man's life until Jesus cast the demon.

The Spirit protects us from being killed by Satan but he is allowed by God to try and deceive us into following him. All the demons will use our weak nature while trying to entice us to the world system that surrounds us. Jesus was talking to some lost people one day and he said: *For you are **the children of your father** the devil, and you love to do the evil things he does. He was a murderer from the beginning. He has always hated the truth, because there is no truth in him. When he lies, it is consistent with his character; for he is a liar and the father of lies. John 8:44* God has given us the righteous Bible and its message is completely empowered by the Spirit. Through the amazing words of God we are equipped to do his work and taught how to accept the power of the Spirit in our everyday life. Christian people know what evil is and must fight it in order to maintain our victory in Jesus. Faith is our victory and it does overcome our enemies.

Salvation is not complete in any of us until the end of our life. We live by faith in the power of God with a solid hope of our next life. The Bible says: *And through your faith, God is protecting you by his power **until you receive this salvation**, which is ready to be revealed on the last day for all to see. 1 Peter 1:5* There is nothing in the Christian life that does not require the power of the Spirit. It is helpful to keep the idea of his power in mind as we go about our daily life. Paul prayed for us and said: *I pray that God, the source of hope, will fill you completely with joy and peace because you trust in him. Then you will overflow with confident hope through **the power of the Holy Spirit.** Romans 15:13* We see here that even our hope is brought to us by the power of the Spirit. Our heartfelt believing is by his power and every time we witness for the Lord to others it is prompted and supported by the same power.

Humans are all born into the powers of this sinful world. This place where we live is covered with evil and this begins with the space that is around the earth. Paul called it the unseen world in this verse: *You used to live in sin, just like the rest of the world, obeying the devil—the commander of the powers in **the unseen world**. Ephesians 2:2a* God created us to be the rulers of this world. Unfortunately Adam listened to Satan and disobeyed the Lord having the result of giving the natural outcome of our life to the Devil. The immediate punishment for this rebellion was to suffer the pains of life and dealing with evil. Even worse is the penalty of Hell. But then our gracious God intervened by sending the Savior to earth and then afterword sent his Spirit at Pentecost. These events when taken by faith can be the most influential things in any human life. Only people that yield to the Spirit of Jesus and allow him to direct their life will ever enter Heaven. The Holy Spirit has the gifts we need to successfully navigate this evil world. God's word have I hid in my heart is something that the Spirit really uses while we are talking to other people.

How can righteous people survive in this evil world that wants to destroy everything that is good or godly? The goal of God is to ultimately defeat all the evil powers that have taken control of this world. None of us has enough power to overcome the Devil and his helpers. This means that we must "trust and obey" wait until we receive the Lord's help. The Spirit of Jesus did join with our own spirit at salvation. This is necessary before we ever win a battle with evil. Paul said it this way: … *if through the power of the Spirit you put to death the deeds of your sinful nature, you will live. For **all who are led** by the Spirit of God are children of God. Romans 8:13-14* This verse is clearly saying that we will live by the Spirit today or we will die eternally. Our victory is faith and the gifts that the Spirit gives each of us. Every believer should depend on the directions of the Spirit in order to live a life that is pleasing to our Father in Heaven.

People who insist on living anyway they want are in rebellion against God. This means that they will live forever in a place of anguish containing all rebellious people. The Scripture says: *The **eyes of the Lord watch over those who do right**, and his ears are open to their prayers. But the Lord turns his face against those who do evil." 1 Peter 3:12* Our Father is not only watching over his family to lead us into righteousness but he is keeping track of every evil person and what they are doing. The Bible says: *So you see, the Lord knows how to rescue godly people from their trials, even while keeping the wicked under punishment until the **day*** *of final judgment. 2 Peter 2:9* Having the gifts of the Spirit is the only way to give us a life that is pleasing to God. The more often we are influenced by the Spirit of Jesus, the quicker we can return to the image of God. Rest assured that the Lord knows who his sheep are.

A sinful human usually does not even realize the jeopardy their life is in. After becoming a Christian we begin to understand that there are many things working against our righteous living. Paul gives us an idea of our opponents: *For we are not fighting against flesh-and-blood enemies, but against evil rulers and authorities of the unseen world, against mighty powers in this dark world, and **against evil spirits** in the heavenly places. Ephesians 6:12* It must be us and the Holy Spirit working together or we don't have a chance of overcoming evil. Today is not only the day of salvation but it is the day of victory for righteousness. Paul was continually encouraging believers to live right: *The night is almost gone; the* (final) *day of salvation will soon be here. So remove your dark deeds like dirty clothes, and put on the shining armor of **right living***. *Romans 13:12* My friends, we must become aware of our enemy before he steals all of our good intentions and leaves us in ruins.

Jesus preached his first great sermon on a mountainside in Israel. If we read it closely it tells us to live a life that is humanly impossible. The only explanation is that Jesus knew the Holy Spirit would come at a later time to live in Christians and then his sermon could have the success and victory that God wants in our life. A born gain person knows that Jesus and the Spirit have the gifts and all the power we need to live completely for God. There are times when we have not because we ask not. Jesus prayed for our victory before he left earth and returned to Heaven: *I'm not asking you to take them out of the world, but to keep them **safe from the evil one.** John 17:15* Today the Lord is asking us to do everything we can to live righteously and reach out to the lost. Remember that believers are called to the most valuable life possible and we want to include others. The Bible says: *Make the most of every opportunity in these evil days. Don't act thoughtlessly, but understand what the Lord wants you to do. Ephesians 5:16-17* The Spirit brings every gift that we need into our life when we are wholehearted.

Paul knew the details of serving Jesus in the Spirit. He said: *A spiritual gift is given to each of us so we can help each other. To one person **the Spirit** gives the ability to give wise advice; to another **the same Spirit** gives a message of special knowledge. **The same Spirit** gives great faith to another, and to someone else **the one Spirit** gives the gift of healing. **He gives** one person the power to perform miracles, **and another** the ability to prophesy. **He gives** someone else the ability to discern whether a message is from the Spirit of God or from another spirit. Still another person **is given** the ability to speak in unknown languages, while another **is given** the ability to interpret what is being said. It is the **one and only Spirit** who distributes all these gifts. **He alone** decides which gift each person should have. 1 Corinthians 12:7-11* All gifts promote the Christian life. Of course a gift will be given to any of God's child at just the right time.

There are some people who will not study Corinthians 12 or 14 although these chapters are part of God's Word. Unfortunately the devil has made many church people afraid of God's spiritual gifts. But the gifts of the Spirit are important because they enable us to help other people. It might help us to learn the groups of gifts. Scholars have divided the gifts from chapter 12 into three parts. They tell us there are three gifts of revelation which are; **wisdom,** knowledge, and discerning of spirits. Next we find three gifts of power which are; **faith,** miracles, and healings. The last three are called the gifts of utterance which are; **prophecy,** tongues, and interpretation. The first gift from each group is believed to be the greatest. Paul said: *But covet earnestly the best gifts:1 Corinthians 12:31a* It is possible that Paul wanted us to seek these three: wisdom, faith, or prophecy. He did tell us that private tongues were the least of the gifts. However any gift is to honor our God.

For two thousand years the Holy Spirit has lived in saved people as our guiding light. He has continually worked in us to build our righteous life and through us to spread the Gospel. The Bible says: *For once you were full of darkness, but now you have light from the Lord. So live as people of light! For this light within **you produces only what is good** and right and true. Ephesians 5:8-9* When we follow the leading of the Spirit and stand firm our godly life is being shaped by the patient Holy Spirit. Another verse says: *But if you remain in me and my words remain in you, you may ask for anything you want, and it will be granted!* **When you produce much fruit,** *you are my true disciples. This brings great glory to my Father. John 15:7-8* Every Christian wants to hear the Lord say "well done faithful servant." This only happens when the Father is able to reward us for the good fruit that we bring into the harvest. This is why the Spirit gives gifts to Christians who will use them for God's work.

The Bible tells us: *There are different kinds of spiritual gifts, but the same Spirit is the source of them all. 1 Corinthians 12:4* The greatest spiritual gift ever given to anyone happened 2000 years ago when God sent the Holy Spirit to overshadow Mary. We were given the human called Jesus who is the only hope of anyone escaping eternal Hell. None of the many gifts of the Spirit would help a Christian without the Savior dying to pay for our sins. We know that the Spirit is part of both Jesus and the Father including eternity past. But now a human family is being built and it will join the trinity in the future eternity. Christians will make a change in eternity and this is the hope of every born-again Christian, belonging to this spiritual union. Jesus made the decision to provide his blood long ago. He is very happy to share his eternal inheritance with us.

The Spirit himself is a huge gift. Every phase of the Spiritual program is administered by him personally for our benefit. The Bible says: *And when he comes, he will convict the world of its sin, and of God's righteousness, and of the coming judgment.* *The* **world's sin** *is that it refuses to believe in me.* **Righteousness is available** *because I go to the Father, and you will see me no more.* **Judgment will come** *because the ruler of this world has already been judged. John 16:8-11* We can observe in this verse that he starts by convicting the world of sin. Jesus told us that righteousness is available through the Spirit. Last of all he tells us that judgment is sure because the Spirit of God already knows exactly every persons ending. The Christian is treated one way and the world is treated differently. When the Spirit is overseeing God's work on earth he never makes one single mistake.

Spiritual gifts are certainly real today if we have enough faith. But they come with a warning that says we are to always put love for others above any other gift. Paul said this: *If I gave everything I have to the poor and even sacrificed my body, I could boast about it; but if I didn't love others, I would have gained nothing. 1 Corinthians 13:3* We learn here that refusing to love others can cost us all our hard work for the Lord. Bringing the Gospel to the lost is our Christian goal and we must learn to do it with love. Love is what turns our hard work into the fruit that God wants from our individual lives. This will allow our small fruit to be multiplied 30 fold or 100 fold by the Spirit working in our life. Chapter 13 of 1 Corinthians is one place to see love discussed by our Christian champion, who is Paul. We must learn that love is the greatest of all!

Jesus and the Holy Spirit love bringing gifts to the Father's family on earth. When Jesus had his perfect victory over the devil and returned to his place in Heaven we were on his mind. Of course he sent the Spirit back to earth to guarantee the needed gifts for our new life. Jesus has followed up ever since with gifts by the billions. The Bible says: *However, he has given each one of us a special gift through the generosity of Christ. That is why the Scriptures say, "When he ascended to the heights, he led a crowd of captives* (we were all captives at one time) ***and gave gifts to his people." Ephesians 4:7-8*** This certainly proves how selfless real love can be. Everything that exists is a gift from the Almighty. The subject of gifts by God is so enormous that no human can possibly do it justice.

Chapter Ten

Great Expectations

*His work is honorable **and glorious**: and his righteousness endures for ever.* Psalm 111:3 (KJV)

Everything God does is glorious. There are many good reasons for this glory. To start with God's glory is from the perfection of a quality character and his magnificence of presence. Glory is the result of absolute truth or real worth of something valuable. Glory consists of things like beauty, power and honor. The creator of all life everywhere is certainly glorious in his actual splendor and magnificence. Each member of the trinity is part of this supreme glory and now they have allowed believers to share in this glory. We should yearn to join in this wondrous glory through the working of the Spirit. Our first taste of this glory actually began long ago when God chose us to be his children before time began. Now we have the opportunity to be born again by the Spirit through our faith and the blood of Jesus. Scriptures tell us: *And we believers also groan, even though we have **the Holy Spirit within us as a foretaste of future glory,** Romans 8:23a* Christians do have great expectations of future glories. We should appreciate the Spirit of Glory as he works in our life restoring us into the image of God.

The Holy Spirit will make the love of God real to a born again Christian. There is no doubt about the glory of God's love. Our human problem is being able to accept this love as our life. Our pride will sometimes hold us back from fully accepting the free gift of love and glory that God offers us. God wants us to love him with everything we have in us. He fully deserves our complete love. If we only accept part of the love he is giving to us it will not be possible for us to return all of our love to him. Being a good person is necessary but this is not complete love for God. We need to have a sincere feeling of love toward the Father each day. A Christian usually feels love toward Jesus because of the terrible price he paid to buy us back from Satan and death. We should also have a love for the Spirit who helps us with our life every day. Love is something that a human possesses that they can freely give to God.

As we share God's glory the reality of what Jesus did by his death and burial starts to sink in. The Christian life we enjoy is because of the Spirit of Glory that Jesus made available to humans two thousand years ago. Scripture tells us: *For God, who said, "Let there be light in the darkness," has made this light shine in our hearts* **so we could know the glory of God** *that is seen in the face of Jesus Christ. 2 Corinthians 4:6* The glory of God completely covers our Savior. Today we have the opportunity to serve the Almighty and tell people about God's glory. Many Christians view their discouragements as some kind of defeat. If we learn to view our set-backs as an opportunity to move toward God then we will be more joyful. Serving Jesus is a wonderful opportunity because we can join with our God and add our tiny bit of effort to glorify the Father. Our reward will be living in the glorious eternal inheritance of Jesus.

Christian hope is based in this "glory" of receiving an eternal inheritance. We never worry that someone will steal our inheritance. We actually invite others to join us because God loves all his children and treats them fairly. Inheritance cannot be earned, it is given: *For you are* **all children of God** *through faith in Christ Jesus. Galatians 3:26* We joined the family by faith in Christ when we were saved from death. At that time the Spirit entered us and becomes the guarantor of our position with God. The Bible says: *And now you Gentiles have also heard the truth, the Good News that God saves you. And when you believed in Christ,* **he identified you as his own** *by giving you the Holy Spirit, whom he promised long ago. Ephesians 1:13* We are told that the Gentiles will receive the same share as a Jew. The Bible recommends that we work hard in our Christianity. This cannot earn our way to Heaven but it shows God that we love him and honor the sacrifices he has made in order to redeem humans.

Our hope of God's glory also includes a new and improved body. When Adam sinned our bodies became much less than they were intended for. The main problem for people is that we were all guaranteed death. This means that a person must receive a different body before they can live eternally with God. All Christians are waiting for the return of Jesus Christ who brings with him the new and improved body that we need to live in God's eternal glory. Paul mentions some of the difference: *Our bodies are buried in brokenness, **but they will be raised in glory.** They are buried in weakness, but they will be raised in strength. 44 They are buried as natural human bodies, but they will be raised as spiritual bodies. For just as there are natural bodies, there are also spiritual bodies. 1 Corinthians 15:43-44* These spiritual bodies are part of the glory of God and are not subject to sin, disease, or death. They will be perfect for the new life we will live with God.

Born again believers in their new bodies will be taken to a brand new world. It will be another wonderful start for humanity without the curse of sin affecting it. This includes a new universe containing a huge earth complete and beautiful. God and his glory will join with humanity when he moves to the new earth to live with us. The Scripture says: *Look! I am creating new heavens and a new earth, and no one will even think about the old ones anymore. Be glad; **rejoice forever in my creation**! And look! I will create Jerusalem as a place of happiness. Her people will be a source of joy. Isaiah 65:17-18* God is building the grandest most beautiful city ever conceived. All God's children will have mansions in that city. John saw the city and said: *... he showed me the holy city, Jerusalem, descending out of heaven from God. It shone with the glory of God and sparkled like a precious stone—like jasper as clear as crystal. Revelation 21:10-11* The glory of God will actually be the beautiful light that fills every corner.

However no one can deny that there will be some tough times while we remain here on earth. Because a Christian's whole life is serving the Lord every one of our problems belongs to Jesus. Of course being part of God's glory is worth any sacrifice we might make. The Bible encourages us by saying: *So be happy when you are insulted for being a*

*Christian, for then **the glorious Spirit of God** rests upon you. 1 Peter 4:14* It is wonderful having the Spirit help us with the difficulties of life. Unbelievers cannot separate us from God, they only make us draw closer to him. We should realize that when we were saved the Spirit of God came into us and brought with him the glory of Jesus. John said: *"I have given them **the glory you gave me**, so they may be one as we are one. John 17:22* We can become one with God! The work of serving Jesus is such a high and glorious calling that life's difficultly is nothing by comparison. Remember, we are not the natural person that we were born. When Jesus became our master his Spirit came in and changed us into a glorious being.

Our hope in the future glory is placed in us by the Spirit as we serve our Savior. It's true that every person has some kind of hope. This world has terrible sinners who will sometimes admit that they hope to go to Heaven. But the hopes of unsaved people have no eternal value. Worthwhile hope is found in a saving relationship with Jesus Christ. Obtaining this special hope in the Savior begins when a person is born-again. Christians know the history of what Jesus did for us at his resurrection. Peter said it in a wonderful way: *All praise to God, the Father of our Lord Jesus Christ. It is by his great mercy that we have been born again, because God raised Jesus Christ from the dead. Now **we live with great expectation,** 1 Peter 1:3* Real hope means that we are living in expectation of a life with God forever. This is very different than the life of a person who has no idea of their future. The Bible says: ... *You lived in this world without God **and without hope**. Ephesians 2:12* Unsaved people don't know how dangerous it is to live without Jesus. Because the Holy Spirit lives in us we can actually feel a powerful hope for our life.

One time while teaching about our glorious life, Paul told us that faith is directly connected to our hope for everything righteous. Before he makes a list of faithful old saints he says: ***Faith is the confidence that what we hope for** will actually happen; it gives us assurance about **things we cannot see**. Hebrews 11:1* In the Old Testament no believer ever saw their faith in the Savior realized. They died hoping that the Redeemer would come to Earth someday and raise them up. But today Jesus has already come the first time and our hope for a Heavenly home is very close. There is a lot more biblical information available and the reality of Heaven has become much clearer. In addition, the Spirit is making Jesus real to each born again Christian. In another Scripture Paul said: ... *from your confident hope of what God has reserved for you in heaven. You have had this expectation ever since you first heard the truth of the Good News. Colossians 1:5* A great spiritual hope comes to us when we serve our Lord. Believers of all times have a hope in God and his eternity. David said long ago "My only hope is in God." Psalm 39:7

God the creator in his mercy has given us the Spirit of Hope. He is everything to the comfort of our righteous life. No human being ever had even an accidental chance of finding their way to Heaven. Many people will not accept that they cannot control the outcome of their life. People must have faith to find Jesus then the hope of Heaven will follow. Paul made it plain about people before salvation: *Live no longer as the Gentiles do, for **they are hopelessly** confused. Ephesians 4:17* He continues by saying our life changes when we learn about the truth of Jesus. The Bible says that our old nature must die so that the Spirit can bring new thoughts and attitudes for us to accept. Our new nature can become more like God who is righteous and holy. There is no confusion in the hope of a born again Christian. Yes, we can become mixed up at times when dealing with our everyday circumstances. But this never affects the absolute hope we have in joining with the glory of God.

The special hope that Christians have gives a spiritual power to our life. John mentions that a believer will have the power to live a pure life. The Bible says: ... *But we do know that we will be like him, for we will see him as he really is. And **all who have this eager expectation** will keep themselves pure, just as he is pure. 1 John 3:2-3* He is referring to the fact that a natural person has no natural ability to make themselves righteous before God. A Christian is receiving the super power provided by the Spirit of Jesus. If we don't feel a desire to be holy every day then something is wrong. Paul reminded one church which had many works that their Savior was the only one responsible for their good works. He said: *As we pray to our God and Father about you, we think of your faithful work, your loving deeds, and the enduring hope you have **because of our Lord Jesus Christ.** 1 Thessalonians 1:3* The Lord gives us our good works and they are always for the glory of God.

The Almighty God created the whole universe with a human family as his goal. We may not know why we were created but it is wonderful for us and Glorious for him. Because of our sin he provided us the plan of salvation. Peter talked about it: *It was the precious blood of Christ, the sinless, spotless Lamb of God. 20 God chose him as your ransom long before the world began, but he has now revealed him to you in these last days. 21 Through Christ you have come to trust in God. And you have **placed your faith and hope in God** because he* (his Spirit) *raised Christ from the dead and gave him great glory. 1 Peter 1:19-21* His plan has brought hope for millions of believers. We are not talking about a natural hope but the eternal hope that a Christian possesses. Because all humans are born with death in their future they cannot have eternal hope. To repeat, God has given a rescue plan to the people of earth and our salvation is the basis of the hope we find in everything a Christian does.

All the abilities and power of the Holy Spirit support this wonderful hope that Christians have to reach glory someday. We will be able to love the people around us because of the Spirit's eternal hope. Paul said: *And **this hope** will not lead to disappointment. For we know how dearly God loves us, because he has given us **the Holy Spirit to fill our hearts** with his love. Romans 5:5* We will never have any disappointment in our hope of living with Jesus in Heaven some day. As we live our lives here on earth it is important that we remember this special hope. If we read the Scriptures every day we will find many wonderful promises that will help our hope to grow stronger. This is what Paul said at the end of one letter: *the **Scriptures give us hope** and encouragement as we wait patiently for God's promises to be fulfilled. Romans 15:4* We must patiently help give other people as much encouragement as possible and accept the Spirit's special hope. The glory of God is certainly waiting for the righteous people from earth.

Our hope of glory is well founded in the Scripture. Jesus led the way as the truth of the Spirit saturated his life here on earth. Here is one well known example that was witnessed: *And as he was praying, the appearance of his face was transformed, and his clothes became dazzling white. Then two men, Moses and Elijah, appeared and began talking with Jesus.* **They were glorious to see.** *And they were* **speaking about his exodus from this world**, *which was about to be fulfilled in Jerusalem. Luke 9:29-31* Every Christian will be leaving this world in a glorious ascension to meet their Savior in the air. Millions of Christians in the air will be quite a glorious sight in its self. When Jesus went to the wedding in Cana he did not seem to know that the Spirit of God would have him begin his miracle ministry. But suddenly he was encouraged to do: *This miraculous sign at Cana in Galilee was* **the first time Jesus revealed his glory**. *And his disciples believed in him. John 2:11* This display convinced his disciples that Jesus was from God.

The same ministry work has been given to Christians today. We are not normally allowed to put on the flashy signs because we would accept the glory of them which would ruin our own spirituality. Jesus tells us that simply completing the work we are assigned is the answer. We read: **I brought glory to you here on earth by completing the work** *you gave me to do. Now, Father, bring me into the glory we shared before the world began. John 17:4-5* It may be hard to believe but we will be joined to this ancient glory someday. The goal of each Christian must be to complete the work that God has called us to do whatever it might be. The Bible says: *Because of our faith, Christ has brought us into this place of undeserved privilege where we now stand, and we confidently and joyfully* **look forward to sharing God's glory**. *Romans 5:2* Reach for the promises my friends, without any doubt, and your joy will be full forever.

For you died to this life, and your real life is hidden with Christ in God. And when Christ, who is your life, is revealed to the whole world, **you will share in all his glory.** Colossians 3:3-4

Conclusion

The plan of God for humans required the seven Spirits, or powers, of God to accomplish the task that saves individuals from eternal sin. God does not explain to us why the Holy Spirit operates the way he does. But the Bible is very clear that we owe our existence to the many works that the Lord gave to the Holy Spirit. Conservative teachers do not think the many wonderful physical creations in our universe are the total meaning of the seven Spirits represented in Heaven. They reason that the seven Spirits are representing the spiritual goodness of God Almighty. There are Scriptures inferring that the power of God is his goodness and righteousness. This includes wisdom, grace, truth, love, holiness, power and glory. These seem to be good divisions for the seven Spirits but we are not actually given a list of the Spirit's work. From our lowly position on earth we naturally worship God for the creation of our life and the wonderful salvation of it.

One way or another we are confident that the power of the Spirit is being poured out during these last days of Christianity in a way that has never been seen. Here is God's plan for Christian's and it is powered by the Holy Spirit: *So we praise God for the glorious grace he has poured out on us who belong to his dear Son. He is so rich in kindness and grace that he purchased our freedom with the blood of his Son and forgave our sins. He has showered his kindness on us, along with all wisdom and understanding. God has now revealed to us his mysterious plan regarding Christ, a plan to fulfill his own good pleasure. **And this is the plan: At the right time he will bring everything together under the authority of Christ—everything in heaven and on earth.** Ephesians 1:6-14* The Holy Spirit will certainly finish all the work that God has asked of him. Today we wait for the soon return of Jesus with the great power to end this age.

Our spirit has been combined with the Spirit of God. This certainly makes us spiritually more powerful than any worldly person could ever be. A Christian does not live in fear of anything. God wants us to develop a confidence in him that will change our life. We act in faith today but soon we will enter the reality of our new world and we will not need faith.

The Bible says: *I also pray that you will understand the incredible greatness of God's **power for us who believe him**. This is the same mighty power that raised Christ from the dead and seated him in the place of honor at God's right hand in the heavenly realms. Ephesians 1:19-20* It is true that unsaved people are exercising their small power in this world today, but like Jesus we live as gentle lambs even while being mistreated. However there is a new world coming soon and the children of God will be rulers with great power forever.

This book is asking you to dedicate yourself to living in the Holy Spirit by allowing him to direct every part of your life. God's desires will come through Jesus to the Spirit and be then given to us. If you are humble and surrendered to Jesus the Spirit will give you knowledge of God's plan for everything in your life. When you are doing his will you will receive the needed power that you would never have had on your own. In a serious matter we can fast and pray which will remove our mind from the things of this world so we can focus on God alone. This will bring us a godly response. Obeying the Spirit will always yield a blessing and following the Spirit will cause you to be a loving person. Paul asked us if we started out following the Spirit then why would we now attempt to run things ourselves.

Here are examples of people who listened to the Holy Spirit:

Acts 8:29 The Holy Spirit said to Philip

Acts 10:19 The Holy Spirit said to him (Peter)

Acts 11:12 The Holy Spirit told me to go with them (Peter)

Acts 11:28 predicted by the Spirit that a great famine was coming (by Agabus)

Acts 13:4 So Barnabas and Saul were sent out by the Holy Spirit

Acts 16:7 again the <u>Spirit of Jesus</u> did not allow them to go there (Paul and Silas)

Everyone who does not accept Jesus and the Spirit will die bodily and then have their soul continue in the place of torment. While in this world the Spirit uses our spiritual power to do the work of God. When we operate in the Spirit's power it is our opportunity to contribute to the Lord's work and show other people the righteous character of God. Paul said it this way: *May you always be filled with the fruit of your salvation —the righteous character produced in your life by Jesus Christ—for this will bring much glory and praise to God. Philippians 1:11* Hopefully, seeing the many things that the Holy Spirit is doing for us, our own faith will be increased. My heart cries out to know and serve God. Our work is to love God first and other people second. The "last days" demand that we seek the power of the Holy Spirit and serve God with our whole heart.

Every Christian waits excitedly for their brand new eternal body. This body will be given to us when Jesus returns to collect his family from off this Earth. This will only happen to Spirit filled people who are serving the Lord. People today are saying that lukewarm believers will make to Heaven some way because God loves everybody. This is not what the Bible says; we must tell them the truth. It will take a great amount of power to place our spirit in a brand new body. The following passage refers to this power of the Spirit: *The Spirit of God, who raised Jesus from the dead, lives in you. And just as God raised Christ Jesus from the dead, he will give life to your mortal bodies **by this same Spirit** living within you. Romans 8:11* Every unsaved person takes their last breath knowing that the darkness of death is waiting for them. If they can think at all they know how powerless they are to change anything. It is very different with a spirit-led Christian. They know that they are going to by-pass death and go directly to live with the Lord. The Spirit is the one who makes this happen.

A day will soon be here when Christians leave this earth and then the whole world will realize the fullness of God's power. The Bible says: *For all creation is waiting eagerly for that future day when God will reveal who his children really are. Romans 8:19* Every born-again person, dead or alive, will meet Jesus in the air for this wonderful ending to Christianity. Paul went on to say: ... *We, too, wait with eager hope for the day when God will give us our full rights as his adopted children,* **including the new bodies** *he has promised us. We were given this hope when we were saved ... Romans 8:23-24* It is exciting to know that a wonderful new body is waiting for us to begin our new eternal life. All the great things that the Spirit does for us are exciting, but his final work of moving us out of this old world into a new world is an absolutely fantastic ending for Christians. Our loving Father has created humans with the potential to actually live in his righteous presence and to relate with the great I AM.

Come soon, Lord Jesus!

Scripture References

1 Peter 2:5
Ephesians 4:11-12
John 7:39
1 Corinthians 12:13
John 14:27
Romans 5:5
Romans 8:26
Ephesians 1:13b-14
Ezekiel 36:26-27
Psalm 119:34-35
Galatians 6:15-16
2 Corinthians 1:20-22
Romans 15:8-9a
Ezekiel 39:27
Zechariah 10:8
Zechariah 13:9
Romans 11:26-27
Ephesians 2:10

Chapter Four The Chosen
Philippians 1:6
Romans 8:15
1 John 3:7-10
Luke 19:10
2 Thessalonians 2:13
Romans 8:11a
Galatians 5:16
1 Corinthians 2:10
2 Corinthians 5:17
Philippians 3:21
Ephesians 4:3-4
1 Thessalonians 4:17

John 14:18-20
Romans 8:15
Galatians 3:27
Titus 3:7
Hebrews 6:17
James 2:5
Ephesians 1:14

Chapter Five God's Will Fulfilled
John 16:10
Romans 12:1
Romans 1:4
Romans 8:13
2 Timothy 3:5
2 Thessalonians 1:11
1 John 4:9-10
Ephesians 3:18-19
1 Corinthians 13:3
Matthew 5:44-45

Chapter Six Conscious of the Spirit
Romans 8:9
1 Corinthians 6:11
2 Thessalonians 2:13
Romans 8:14
Romans 6:6-7
Colossians 2:20a
Romans 6:4
2 Corinthians 3:17
Ephesians 4:23-24
1 Peter 4:14
Acts 21:10-14

1 Peter 1:5
Romans 6:8
Romans 6:16
Romans 8:28

Chapter Seven *God's Vital Wisdom*
Acts 9:17
2 Chronicles 5:11-14
Hebrews 10:4
John 15:26-27a
Acts 2:38
Acts 2:4
Acts 5:32
1 Corinthians 12:27
Hebrews 3:13-15
1 Thessalonians 4:16-18
Acts 20:28
Colossians 3:16
James 5:13-15
Galatians 6:2,3
Ephesians 4:13
Acts 4:31
John 4:23
Ephesians 2:18
Romans 5:10
Philippians 3:3
1 Thessalonians 5:16-19

Chapter Eight *Wisdom for Our New Life*
James 3:17
Luke 2:40
Acts 6:3

Luke 21:14-15
1 Corinthians 1:24
1 Thessalonians 1:5
1 Peter 1:10-12
Revelation 19:6
Ephesians 6:18
Jude 1:20-21
1 Peter 4:12-14
1 Corinthians 3:16-17
Luke 19:37 Psalm 31:7
Luke 4:14
Luke 4:18-19
Luke 3:16
2 Corinthians 6:10
Philippians 4:5-6
Psalm 21:1-2
Psalm 31:7
Psalm 33:1
John 7:39
2 Corinthians 5:4b-5
Acts 11:28
Acts 13:2
Acts 16:7
Isaiah 30:21

Chapter Nine *Magnificent Gifts*
Acts 19:1-7
Acts 8:12-17
2 Corinthians 12:12
Romans 12:6-8
2 Timothy 1:6-7
1 John 4:18-19

John 14:12
Acts 10:38
Hebrews 13:8
1 Corinthians 14:32
John 3:5-6
John 1:33
2 Timothy 1:6
John 14:12
1 Peter 5:8-9
Matthew 9:32-33
John 8:44
1 Peter 1:5
Romans 15:13
Ephesians 2:2a
Romans 8:13-14
1 Peter 3:12
2 Peter 2:9
Ephesians 6:12
Romans 13:12
John 17:15
Ephesians 5:16-17
1 Corinthians 12:7-11
1 Corinthians 12:31a
Ephesians 5:8-9
John 15:7-8
1 Corinthians 12:4
John 16:8-11
1 Corinthians 13:3
Ephesians 4:7-8

Chapter Ten *Great Expectations*

Psalm 111:3
Romans 8:23a
2 Corinthians 4:6
Galatians 3:26
Ephesians 1:13
1 Corinthians 15:43-44
Isaiah 65:17-18
Revelation 21:10-11
1 Peter 4:14
John 17:22
1 Peter 1:3
Ephesians 2:12
Hebrews 11:1
Colossians 1:5
Psalm 39:7
Ephesians 4:17
1 John 3:2-3
1 Thessalonians 1:3
1 Peter 1:19-21
Romans 5:5
Romans 15:4
Luke 9:29-31
John 2:11
John 17:4-5
Romans 5:2
Colossians 3:3-4

Conclusion

Ephesians 1:6-14
Ephesians 1:19-20
Acts 8:29

Acts 10:19
Acts 11:12
Acts 11:28
Acts 13:4
Acts 16:7
Philippians 1:11
Romans 8:11
Romans 8:19
Romans 8:23-24